Are You Judging Me Yet?

Poetry and Everyday Sexism

for Mum and Dad

Are You Judging Me Yet?

Poetry and Everyday Sexism

Kim Moore

SEREN

is the book imprint of
Poetry Wales Press Ltd.
Suite 6, 4 Derwen Road, Bridgend,
Wales, CF31 1LH

www.serenbooks.com
facebook.com/SerenBooks
twitter: @SerenBooks

ISBN 978-1-78172-687-7

A CIP record for this title is available
from the British Library.

The publisher works with the financial
assistance of the Books Council of Wales.

Cover artwork: 'Reclining Nocturne 1', 2015, cast glass, 21.5 x 53 x 32.5 inches.
© Karen LaMonte. Photography by Martin Polak.

Printed by Severn, Gloucester.

Contents

FOREWORD

This book started its life as a PhD thesis at Manchester Metropolitan University, where I worked under the supervision of Professor Michael Symmons Roberts, Dr Nikolai Duffy and Dr Angelica Michelis.

It's a text that has already undergone a transformation. Part of it is currently living another life as my second collection of poems *All the Men I Never Married*, published by Seren in 2021. This is its second transformation, as a reader-directed text, consisting of seventeen sections of prose, five groups of poems and two individual poems, one at the beginning of the book and one at the end. Although it can be read in a linear fashion, and will make sense when approached in this way, you are invited to make your way through the book by selecting from several options that appear at the bottom of each section. These choices, or textual signposts will allow you to chart your own desired paths through the text, deciding as you go along what you would like to read next.

Since this text is in conversation with *All the Men I Never Married*, I hope that readers will want to continue onwards to my poetry collection to read the rest of the poems, but perhaps also to meet the poems they have encountered here in that new context. I've always wanted to write a book that sends the reader out from between its pages and into other books, other worlds, and I hope this book does that.

While I hope that readers will make journeys outward from the book, *Are You Judging Me Yet?* is for me, as its author, a book about what it is like to be a woman, and a poet, and a performer of poetry, in this particular time and place and body I have found myself in, at the very beginning of a millennium.

The young people I work with still experience sexism. A teenage girl told me that a teacher said to her 'If I'm blushing your skirt's too short'. What does this tell teenage girls about men and who is responsible for their behaviour? What gives me hope is not that anything has changed since I was a young woman, but that these young women have the language to articulate what is happening to them.

I wanted this book to have a purpose, to add to discussions around feminism and sexism and to talk about how it feels to be a female poet. I wanted to highlight the role lyric poetry can play in such discussions. I wanted to write a playful, angry, sad, thoughtful, transforming, transformative book – and by reading it you are transforming it once again: for that act of faith I give my thanks.

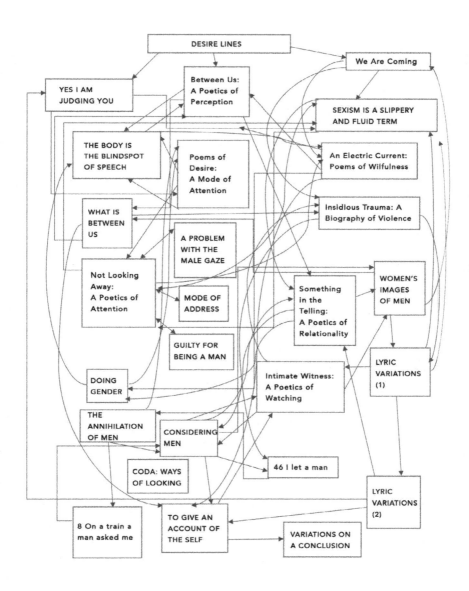

DESIRE LINES:
VARIATIONS ON AN INTRODUCTION

1.

If choices are threaded through the body of a text – if the text is not a body – but a landscape – if the text is a landscape – there must be paths – if there is one path – there is always another – if text is a landscape – with paths running through – then reading is a form of travel – if reading is a form of travel – readers must be travellers – some of them will know where they are going – some will be lost –

if text is a landscape – if reading is a form of travel – if readers are travellers – then the text is a journey in itself – if the text is a journey and a landscape – if all landscapes have paths – if each path is a choice – a desire – if this text has its own desires – there are bodies within it – yours and mine – we may find ourselves meeting somewhere inside –

2.

This book aims to create a space for new ways of thinking about sexism and the role it plays in society. When I started writing poems about sexism, back in 2016, there was not much discussion of sexism in UK poetry as a force in and of itself, and certainly no book length considerations of it.

There are of course, many poets writing about related forms of gender-based violence and trauma. Moniza Alvi,

Helen Ivory and Pascale Petit have been particularly in-
fluential on my thinking. Ivory's excellent *Waiting for
Bluebeard* examines the impact of domestic violence, using
a well-known fairy tale as a lens. Petit's collections incorpor-
ate vivid and surreal descriptions of rainforests and the
natural world to reflect on trauma and child abuse, whilst
Alvi's *Europa* is one of the most beautiful and perfectly
poised explorations of post-traumatic stress disorder I've
ever read.

I wanted to write about everyday sexism, but swiftly came
to realise that sexism is not so easily categorised. Often what I
thought I was writing about was different to what I ended up
with.

In 2015, my first full-length poetry collection *The Art of
Falling* was published by Seren, containing a sequence of
seventeen poems called 'How I Abandoned My Body to His
Keeping' which examine a personal experience of domestic
violence.

After ten years of not speaking about what happened, of
pretending that nothing happened, the poems were not so
much an attempt to tell a story or represent a truth. Instead
they became repositories of meaning for me – a way of creat-
ing a narrative. However fragmented, however broken that
narrative was – by both the passage of time and the strange
things our brains do to process traumatic events, I was deter-
mined to use the framework of poetry to attempt to contain
what had happened to me. I had no interest in a chronological
or linear sequence – because the experience was not linear for
me. But I did want to resolve it somehow, and decided that the
locked box of a sonnet at the end of the sequence would be
the perfect form to to do this, and hopefully stop my thoughts
returning to the subject again. From the vantage point of over
five years later, I see this impulse was a little naïve, but it was
what I needed to tell myself to be able to write and finish the
sequence.

Violent relationships are marked by the act of transformation.

The perpetrator transforms – from loving to violent, and the victim is transformed also. I spent a lot of time reading Ovid's *Metamorphosis* to try and understand this. Rape and violence are at the heart of so many of these myths, but so is transformation – both as something forced on someone, but also as a means of survival, a means of escape.

The transformation of the self by another in a violent relationship seems to me to be the most violent thing that can happen, in terms of its long-term, insidious effects. The poems in 'How I Abandoned My Body To His Keeping' are full of acts of transformation. Bodies become pillars of smoke, minds become empty tables, hearts become monuments. A man is made smaller and smaller until he is so tiny he becomes pervasive, part of the air needed to breathe. One speaker turns into a bird, another into Europa before she is abducted and raped by Zeus.

The question often asked of people who are in violent relationships – 'Why do you stay?' – or if they have managed to escape – 'Why did you stay so long?' – has always haunted me, perhaps partly because I kept asking this question of myself. *All the Men I Never Married* is in part, an attempt to answer this question, building on the work I started in *The Art of Falling*, as I became convinced that less egregious forms of sexism are in some sense the foundation upon which the worst forms of gendered violence are built.

Living in a body that experiences everyday sexism is like receiving hundreds and hundreds of tiny paper cuts in such a way as to make this seem normal, and how can this not make someone more vulnerable to being in a violent relationship? I began to realise that the answer to the question – 'Why did you stay?' – can't just be found in examining what happened, but also in the examination of the political, social and historical conditions that created the possibility of it happening in the first place.

3.

I started to write poems about men, not realising that writing men (plural) was an uncovering of female desire, an admitting to female desire, and that this was risky business, that this uncovering sometimes meant that the sexism that was already in the room, perhaps in hiding, was emboldened to show itself, to speak up.

The female desire I became interested in articulating is characterised by distance and absence, by lack and longing. A female desire found in both the insistence of the gaze, but also its restlessness, a female desire found in the space between two people, a female desire that is not loyal, a female desire that sits back on its haunches and observes, that sometimes steps back behind language when sexism enters the room.

4.

Halfway through my PhD I attended a training session on creative-critical research, which was useful, but did not lift the rising sense of panic I felt when I thought about actually writing my thesis. The lecturer said that if any of the participants would like to meet afterwards for an informal chat about their work, we should email her and she would meet us for a coffee.

So I got in touch and we arranged to meet in the university cafeteria. She asked me what my main methodology was. I remember putting my head in my hands in despair, and replying 'this is the problem. I'm finding it impossible to stick to one. I'm taking bits from all over the place to say what I want to say. I can't seem to stop.' She smiled and said 'That's bricolage methodology.' And in that moment I understood all over again the importance of naming.

N.K. Denzin writes that bricolage is a 'complex, dense, reflective, collage-like creation that represents the researcher's images, understandings and interpretations of the world or phenomena under analysis.'[1] Bricolage allows me to use disparate paradigms such as feminist theory, lyric theory, film theory and close reading to illuminate my own thinking. D. Weinstein and M.A. Weinstein argue that bricolage allows us to 'connect the parts to the whole, stressing the meaningful relationships that operate in the situations and social worlds studied.'[2]

5.

During my research, I performed the poems that I was writing about sexism, and then these performances became part of the research as I reflected on exchanges, reactions and conversations with audience members. This led me to research mode of address in lyric poetry, which led me to Judith Butler and what happens when we address another, when we give an account of ourselves, which led me to thinking about desire, but also trauma. Except this description of the research process is not accurate at all, because these things did not lead to each other in a linear fashion, but instead happened simultaneously, encompassing and touching and brushing up against each other.

Bricolage is both a methodology and a made thing – as Denzin points out, it is a 'collage-like creation' that should represent the researcher's 'understandings and interpretations of the world'[3]. I realised that a traditionally structured PhD thesis, separated into a 'creative' and 'critical' section with chapters would not fit my growing understanding of the complexity of writing lyric poetry about sexism.

Similarly, a traditionally constructed book of essays which did not hold a space for my poetry and the way it has fed into and developed my thinking around the complexity of living in a society where sexism is both dynamic and embedded, would not work, would not be a living, transforming, transformative creature-book in the way I needed it to be.

6.

The reader-directed format of this book takes its inspiration from the *Fighting Fantasy* adventure series of role-playing gamebooks which were huge favourites of my childhood. These books made the reader a protagonist in the story and gave them agency to make decisions about how they made their way through the text, giving an element of control over the narrative.

The *Fighting Fantasy* gamebooks had specific rules and a complex system which used dice to establish key factors such as the 'Strength', 'Skill' and 'Luck' of the reader/player. An 'Adventure Sheet' at the front of the book allowed the player to record these ongoing figures, with the scores having a huge impact on how the reader made their way through the text and how easily they completed their adventure. These books bend genre, so they exist as both narrative and game. The textual element (to my teenage self at least) is a satisfying and coherent narrative but the existence of both the rules and a right and wrong way of progressing through the text situate them just as firmly in the gaming genre.

Instead of an 'Adventure Sheet', I've incorporated three different starting points to this book, depending on how the reader most closely identifies – as male, female, or non-binary. These three options are narrow because of practical considerations and I know they will not cover the wide and varied spectrum of how all people identify, but I hope that giving this option at the beginning emphasises that all reading is an act of interpretation, and one that we take part in whilst being situated in our experience of gender (amongst other identities such as class, race, sexuality etc).

Whereas there was a real risk of the protagonist 'dying' when reading a *Fighting Fantasy* gamebook and having to start again, the reader of this book can make their way through the text safely, with nothing more alarming happening than being looped around to re-read a particular text for the second or even third time.

Many *Fighting Fantasy* books encouraged the reader to make a map to ensure they did not get lost. Some were impossible to finish without drawing a detailed map. Getting lost, getting frustrated and having to start again was part of the process, part of the fun of these books.

I have included a map at the beginning of this book. It's intended as a visual aid to you, the reader, to show all of the possible paths through and the connections that I've made between sections. Instead of a gamesheet, I've included a 'Reader Checklist' (page 186) at the end of the book that you can use (if you want to) to ensure you haven't missed anything out.

There are no rules and there's no right or wrong way of moving through this book – so it's not a game in the same sense that the *Fighting Fantasy* gamebooks are. I've not incorporated any use of dice or chance elements to direct your movement through the text. However, you are offered choices to allow you to progress, and these choices will take you in different directions – a feature in common with the *Fighting Fantasy* series.

The *Fighting Fantasy* gamebooks use the pronoun 'you' throughout the text. This unusual mode of address is necessary to directly address the reader and ask them to select a path. It also allows the reader to identify as a character within the book. The choices at the end of each section of text in the *Fighting Fantasy* gamebooks are also directly addressed to the reader. They use a repetitive structure – they always start with the words 'If you.' For example, in *Trial of Champions*, by Ian Livingstone, one set of choices is 'If you wish to pick up the silver box, turn to 224. If you would rather climb down the ladder and carry on walking up the tunnel, turn to 361.'

I've tried, as much as possible, to replicate this repetitive sentence structure, whilst incorporating playfulness through direct address and questions addressed to readers in the choices at the end of each section of text. Sometimes I ask the reader what they would like to read next, but at other times ask the reader to choose what to read based on their reaction or feeling about what they've just read, or based upon their own previous life experiences. In this way, I hope to provoke, encourage and challenge the reader to confront their own connectedness or distance from the text that they have read.

7.

I have included poems grouped in twos and sometimes threes, but always prefaced by a title, or what I think of as a doorway, which indicates to the reader the lens through which to read these poems. For example, one group of poems is called 'An Electric Current: Poems of Wilfulness'. This title invites the reader to read wilfulness into these poems, or to read them for wilfulness. However, some of these poems could just as easily move into a different grouping. These doorway titles are there to encourage the reader to both move with, and push back against the way the poems have been categorised.

There is a path that can be taken to read only poetry, or only prose, which will create a different reading experience than if the reader passes from one to the other. It's impossible for me to predict what effect the different reading routes will have on a reader – the only way of knowing that is to give each one a go.

8.

When I first started writing this book, I thought readers would create their own desire path, or desire line through the text. Desire paths are defined by Robert Macfarlane on Twitter in his 'Word of the Day' (March 25th, 2018) as 'paths & tracks made over time by the wishes & feet of walkers, especially those paths that run contrary to design or planning.' I hoped that these paths of desire would generate new meanings, new interpretations, a new text.

Now I realise the paths of desire are mine, traces of my thinking, my reading. My desire paths weave the creative and the critical together, and then pull them apart. They invite the reader to think about how they can move through a book, and why they move in the way they do.

The easiest path is to read in a linear fashion, from beginning to end. This is the path of least resistance. If a reader chooses to follow a desire path, to move back and forward through these pages, through this text, then they become implicated in the text, through their choice of what to read next, or what not to read. When the reader follows my desire paths, creating their own desire path in turn, they may produce something the writer cannot control. The text becomes what Roland Barthes calls a 'text of bliss' – a text that:

> imposes a state of loss, the text that discomforts (perhaps
> to the point of boredom), unsettles the reader's historical,
> cultural, psychological assumptions, the consistency of his
> tastes, values, memories, brings to a crisis his relation
> with language[4]

9.

Instead of a desire path, call it a sightline, a line of sight. If what John Berger says is true, that '[W]e only see what we look at. To look is an act of choice'[5], then by making this choice explicit in the text, readers are forced to confront and question what they choose to look at or not to look at. This shift away from authorial control allows a collaboration to develop between the reader and the text, where the reader actively constructs the texts and narratives rather than passively consumes them.

John Berger argued that '[t]he meaning of an image is changed according to what one sees immediately beside it or what comes immediately after it.'[6] This book sets out to show that this is also an accurate way of understanding how texts communicate, particularly poetry, where the placing and ordering of poems can be extremely important in the way readers interpret and understand the wider narrative of a collection.

The desire paths through this book, these sightlines, may create a different trajectory and a different landscape for the reader to move through. Think of it as an unfolding, where each sightline, each desire path gives the reader a different view on the one that came before and the one that is to come. Think of it as a circling back round.

10.

If there is no correct way through a text, but only multiple configurations of how that text can be read and experienced, this is a challenge both to the idea of the reader as a passive consumer, and the writer as the importer of knowledge. A text which contains choices within it moves towards an idea of the reader and writer being implicitly connected and bound up with each other and makes this explicit.

Discussing the work of Judith Butler, Sarah Salih writes that:

> In this sense, "to live" as Butler defines it, is to live a life politically – in other words, to recognise one's relation to others, one's relation to power, and one's responsibility to strive for a collective, more inclusive future.[7]

How can the act of reading embody these values? Can texts encourage the reader to think about power – not just through the content they explore, but through the form this content takes? Can the structure of a text encourage a reader to think about and recognise their relation to power as well as their relation to others? If texts embody and enact choice (and with any choice, power is inherent) can this bring both reader and writer closer to what it means to live a political life?

Sarah Salih points out that Butler's commitment to the 'withholding of reassuring answers' in her work is not difficulty for the sake of difficulty or obscurity, but a 'political mode that is designed to produce a sense of alienation and discomfort in the reader so that newness may enter and alter a defamiliarized world.'[8] In an interview with Gary A. Olson and Lynn Worham in 2000 in which Butler discussed the move in academic writing towards what she called 'radical accessibility', she argued for 'an analysis of the kinds of occlusions or concealments that take place when we take ordinary language to be a true indicator of reality as it is and as it must be.'[9]

Although I am sympathetic to Butler's viewpoint, and agree with it to a certain extent, I do not see 'radical accessibility' as a bad thing, if the word accessibility is opened up and questioned. There are many different ways of making a text accessible, and not all of them have to be about simplifying language or meaning.

In its interweaving of poetry and prose, this book challenges the traditional ways we have of consuming these two genres, turning the act of reading into an active, participatory experience. It makes its own experiments with producing a sense of alienation and discomfort, with bringing newness into the world and defamiliarizing what is known. One of the reasons I chose to write in this format is in my own starting point. The language of both academia and poetry are strange to my family. As well as being the first in my family to go to university, I am also the first to make a living as a freelance writer and poet. The freedom to pass between poetry and prose, to shift from an academic mode to a poetic mode if needed feels like radical accessibility, and it's something I welcome and embrace.

I hope this book is both radically accessible and alienating, discomforting and recognizable, new and repetitive, all at the same time.

11.

The term 'defamiliarization' was first coined by Viktor Shklovksy in 1917. Using Tolstoy as an example, he outlined different strategies used in literature to defamiliarize the text and in doing so enable the reader to see the world differently. These included describing an event as if it is happening for the first time, avoiding the accepted names for something and naming the corresponding parts of other objects instead, changing the form of an object or action without changing its nature, speaking from an unexpected point of view and lastly to see things and describe them as removed from their normal context.[10]

T. Bennett argued that Shklovsky and other Russian Formalists believed that literature and texts could be used to 'dislocate our habitual perceptions of the real world so as to make it the object of a renewed attentiveness'[11] whilst Daniel P. Gunn states that 'To produce an effect of defamiliarization, then, an artist must consciously violate the accepted ways of making meanings – whatever they are.'[12]

The use of desire paths and choices threaded throughout this book and the encouragement to the reader to progress through the text in a non-linear fashion is intended to violate the accepted ways of making meanings. All of these things change the traditional form of a book without making it completely unrecognisable. The conventional and widely accepted way of making meaning from a text, particularly in prose is the reader reading in a chronological and linear fashion, building on their knowledge and frame of reference as they go. The circular nature of this book is both a subversion and a challenge to this way of making meaning.

Another way of utilizing the technique of defamiliarization is to group the poems under headings such as 'Poems of Desire: A Mode of Attention' or 'Insidious Trauma: A Biography of Violence.' Although best-selling poetry anthologies such as Bloodaxe's *Staying Alive* series group poems under thematic sections, it is usually frowned upon for a poet in a single-authored collection to explicitly 'tell' the reader what a poem is about, so grouping the poems in this way felt risky.

My aim was to create a doorway into the poems, but also to call into question in the mind of the reader whether the label I assign to the poems is suitable, and to invite readers to think about whether some poems would be better placed elsewhere. The reader will be confronted with the impossibility of saying what a poem is really about, and the possibility that a poem could be about different things, at different times, on different days, or maybe even on different readings within the same day or hour.

I hope that the titles of these small groups of poems function like coloured panes of glass that a reader can use to hold a poem up to a different light.

I return to John Berger. I think about what we choose to look at. I think about looking, and choice, and paying attention. I think about noticing things, which can also be a way of dislocating perceptions, how these titles are a way of drawing the reader's attention to something – the desire in the poems, the violence in the poems. I think about how when we draw attention to something, its opposite also comes into view, waiting for us to notice it as well.

12.

In *Living a Feminist Life,* Sara Ahmed points out that 'noticing becomes a form of political labour'[13]. When I began to think about sexism, I noticed it more and more. When I began to think about sexism, I remembered more and more of it happening to me and around me. The noticing of sexism began to defamiliarize the world because it was not the world I thought it was. Whereas Shklovsky's idea of defamilarisation seems to be that literature can make us see the world anew, it was the act of noticing that made me see the world differently. In writing about this, I went back to Shklovsky's list of the ways of defamiliarizing, and decided to experiment with describing incidents of sexism as they were and removing them, at least partly, from their context. The context I removed was the passing of time – I decided to place each incident next to each other without referencing how much time had passed between them. This allowed me to 'defamiliarise' the experience and acts of sexism themselves and understand them as part of a structure, a pattern, a series.

Both sexism and my perception of the world in which I moved through became defamiliarized. As Ahmed explains: '[t]he past is magnified when it is no longer shrunk. We make things bigger just by refusing to make things smaller.'[14] I place sexism in a poem. It does not make it smaller.

Ahmed also points out that '[w]e need structure to give evidence of structure.'[15] I can create a micro-structure of a poem to give evidence. I can use the scaffolding of line breaks and words lined up like bricks in a wall. But I can also use the macro structure of a poetry collection to give evidence, which is more like a body than a building. A body of work. A structure to give evidence of structure.

13.

Sara Ahmed wrote that '[w]e all have different biographies of violence'[16]. I am interested in what a biography of violence would look like. How one biography of violence can hide another. Behind the experience of domestic violence, behind this biography, lies another biography of violence, which led me to that place. Ahmed asks '[w]hat do we do when these kinds of things happen? Who do we become?'[17] To these questions I would add: who do we become when we choose to look, or look away? Who do we become when we speak, or stay silent, or write about the moments we stayed silent?

14.

The knowledge I am drawing from to write this book comes from my own experience of being white, working-class and university-educated. Whilst this concrete experience can and will be used to draw wider conclusions about society and the place of women as an oppressed group, it is important to note that it is impossible to represent all women's experiences with my own. Each woman's experience of sexism and female desire is shaped and influenced by race, class, sexuality, education and disability amongst other multiple variables. This book can only hope to shine one light onto this complex and multifaceted experience.

15.

D. Soyini Madison writes that performance 'illuminates like good theory. It orders the world and lets the world loose'[18]. I read this and realise that I can't predict or determine what will happen when I perform poems about sexism and female desire. Sexism might be conjured into the room or, more accurately, uncovered. I realise that I've started to welcome this release – that I want to 'let the world loose.'

In the performing of poetry around sexism and female desire, I realised I needed to approach each performance with a commitment to being 'challenged, changed, embraced and interrogated in the performance process.'[19] This was something I began to aim for, every time I read. Sometimes it happened during the performance. Sometimes it happened afterwards when engaging with audiences and readers. I realised that performing poetry was a dynamic exchange and could lead to transformation and change for all parties involved.

One of the most important goals of effective autoethnography, in both writing and performance is transformation in the researcher/writer and the audience or reader. Using lyric poetry as autoethnographic scholarship and performances of lyric poems as performative autoethnography became an integral and essential part of my practice, allowing me to reflect and create new work from the discourse and reactions that arose in both myself as a researcher, creative writer and performer and from the reader or audience.

If you identify as a woman, turn to 'Yes, I Am Judging You' on page 28.
If you identify as a man, turn to 'We Are Coming' on page 26.
If you identify as non-binary, or your identity is not covered by these descriptions, turn to 'Between-Us: A Poetics of Perception' on page 71.

WE ARE COMING

We are coming under cover of darkness,
with our strawberry marks, our familiars,
our third nipples, our ill-mannered bodies,
our childhoods spent hobbled like horses

where we were told to keep our legs closed,
where we sat in the light of a window and posed
and waited for the makers of the world
to tell us again how a woman is made.

We are arriving from the narrow places,
from the spaces we were given, with our curses
and our spells and our solitude, with our potions
we swallow to shrink us small as insects

or stretch us into giants, for yes, there are giants
amongst us, we must warn you. There will be riots,
we're carrying all that we know about silence
as we return from the forests and towers,

unmaking ourselves, stepping from the pages
of books, from the eye of the camera, from the cages
we built for each other, the frames of paintings,
from every place we were lost and afraid in.

We stand at the base of our own spines
and watch tree turn to bone and climb
each vertebra to crawl back into our minds,
we've been out of our minds all this time,

our bodies saying no, we were not born for this,
dragging the snare and the wire behind us.

If you are unsure whether sexism exists turn to 'Sexism is a Slippery and Fluid Term' on page 76.

If you would like to read about wilfulness, turn to 'An Electric Current: Poems of Wilfulness' on page 129.

If you would like to read a biography of violence, turn to 'Insidious Trauma: A Biography of Violence' on page 100.

YES, I AM JUDGING YOU

It's November, and mist has swallowed the grounds of the hotel. It's the type of mist that leaves drops of water clinging to your hair and clothes, the type of grey November day that blurs the boundary between sea and sky. I'm here at a hotel in the Lake District as an after-dinner speaker for a luncheon club. Their booked speaker cancelled with only a day's notice, so instead of a talk about knife crime in Manchester, the unsuspecting luncheon club members will receive a poetry reading, whether they like it or not.

I begin with a poem called 'All The Men I Never Married', a list poem which reels off man after man using one sentence descriptions to define their character, their appearance. At the mid-point of the poem, I read the line 'are you surprised, are you judging me yet?' An elderly woman two tables from the front, her knife and fork crossed neatly in front of her, shouts 'Yes!' People around me laugh. I laugh, and my laughter takes me by surprise, because part of me thinks it is funny, and part of me is mortified. There is something funny and not funny about this moment.

> There was the boy who I met on the park
> who tasted of humbugs and wore
> a mustard yellow jumper

The poem relates the sexual history of a speaker and puts it on public display. It runs the risk of oversimplifying the men included within it through the summing up of their characters with one or two sentences. The white space of the poem, which translates into pauses in the performance, leave room for judgement, for interruption.

John Berger's insistence that '[t]o look is an act of choice'[20] runs through my mind every time I perform this poem. I am choosing in this poem to look at men, to be the wielder of the gaze, to make men the gazed upon, which feels risky, which feels dangerous. To look, and not to look away. To look at one man, then another, then another. To let them disappear, which they do as the poem finishes. But they also do not, because once they are spoken of, they are conjured into existence:

> *the kickboxer with beautiful long brown hair*
> *that he tied with a band at the nape of his neck*

After my performance at a festival, another poet tells me she enjoyed my reading, and then says 'I'm sure you know exactly what you're doing. Reading poems about men with your legs out.' She says this in front of another poet, a man, who smirks. I laugh because I don't know what to say. Laughter is the tool I always reach for in moments of discomfort. Later, I wonder what the moment would have felt like if I hadn't laughed, if I'd waited, if I'd held myself still. But by the time I consider this, the moment has passed, the conversation has moved on.

In *Gendering Poetry*, Vicki Bertram argues that women poets, in any performance of their work, have to 'confront the implications of being a female on public display, with the connotations of sexual objectification...'[21]. The female body never passes by unremarked, least of all in the space of a poetry reading. No matter how much I wish it, language can't stand between my body and the world, can't protect me from being confronted by a person who wants to put me in my place, to remind me I am a body, and not a poet.

> *the one with a constant ear infection*
> *so I always sat on his left*

That evening in my hotel room, I lie in bed and look at the ceiling fan whirring lazily above me. The room is about the size of the ground floor of my house. There are floor-to-ceiling curtains which I've only opened once since I arrived, and birds which sound as if they're living behind the bathroom wall. Every morning I'm woken up by the panicked fluttering of wings, or dull thuds. At first, I thought the birds were trapped – now I think there is a nest there, and fledglings not quite ready to fly.

> *the trumpet player I loved*
> *from the moment I saw him*
> *dancing to the Rolling Stones*

I think about Judith Butler, and her assertion that 'to be injured by speech is to suffer a loss of context'[22]. I know she's talking about hate speech, and I'm talking about a woman commenting on my legs, but I remember my cheeks burning, and how, in that moment, I felt like a body, not a person, certainly not a poet.

At the same festival, there was a male poet who the female poets started to call 'The Monster' because of the way he behaved – his hands snaking around you when he'd had a drink in the evening or standing too close at the bar. Every time I finished performing and left the stage, he would be there waiting. Every time he would tell me 'You are so beautiful!' After the fifth time I snapped 'Do you mean my poetry?' He looked startled that I hadn't just said 'Thank you.' I stomped away, feeling guilty and irritated, and a little wild, all at the same time.

Can any language that causes the listener to suffer a loss of context be deemed what Judith Butler calls an 'injurious address'? When a book review mentions the author's photo and the shade of the author's lipstick in what is supposed to be a discussion of their work, the loss of context is the delaying or side-lining of a meaningful engagement with the work itself.

At a recent reading, the organiser commented on my author photo, on the back of my second collection. I am leaning against a tree, looking sideways at the camera. 'That's a bit seductive,' he said. I replied 'Only if you fancy trees.'

and the guy who smoked weed
and got more and more paranoid
whose fingers flickered and danced
when he talked

I return again to that grey November day, the mist coming in from the sea and obscuring everything outside so that the drive leads to nothing, to nowhere, a blankness. The mist is so sure of itself I start to doubt there is anything still there inside it. Maybe everything really has vanished. I know if I walk down to the shore I won't see the signs telling me the sands are treacherous. They have been swallowed up by the mist. I won't see the gulls, tracing the length of the promenade. Anything in the distance is blurred, out of focus, but close up, each of the benches that line the gravel path are laced with spider webs, and everything glistens.

the one whose eyes were two pieces
of winter sky

What do I say with my body when I am performing? I am writing poems about sexism and female desire. When I read poems about sexism, what does my body say about sexism? When I read poems about female desire, what does my body say about female desire?

a music producer
long-legged and full of opinions

I am speaking about sexism, and maybe my body tells of desire. I am speaking about desire, and maybe my body calls sexism into the room.

and more trumpet players
one who was too short and not him
one who was too thin and not him

I am back there again, halfway through the poem. I have listed the men. I am feeling almost tender towards them. I read the question.

are you judging me yet, are you surprised?

An elderly woman shouts 'yes'. Something in me delights in her forthrightness, her not-holding-back. Something in me is deeply ashamed. I laugh with delight and with shame. Both of these things can be true. In the corner of the room, a waiter struggles to open a window. Although it is cold and damp outside, the radiators throughout the hotel are locked on full. The combination of bodies, hot food and the radiators have made the air steamy and the windows fog up.

When Butler writes that the body is 'sustained and threatened through modes of address'[23], it is my body and yours she is talking of. The bodies of audiences and readers can be both sustained and threatened by poetry that addresses them directly, that asks them a question.

Let me tell you of the ones I never kissed
or who never kissed me

I did not understand when I wrote the poem that by addressing the audience with that direct question (are you judging me yet, are you surprised?) I was inviting the body of the other to be vulnerable to address. I do not understand or know any of this until months later, through writing about it again. I learn that written into the poem is the possibility and the space to understand something about power, who has it and who does not.

the trombonist I went drinking with
how we lay in each other's beds
like two unlit candles

That question becomes a radical act – it destabilises my authority as poet by inviting dialogue with and response from the reader/listener. My question also destabilises the audience because it moves away from the conventional form of a poetry reading, a place where, according to Vicki Bertram, audiences can expect to receive 'wisdom and perception distilled by the skill of the wordsmith'[24] into a place where there is space left for interaction. Performance is realised as a living art form, that will be different every time, dependent as it is upon the audience's participation in some form.

> *we were not for each other and in this we were wise*
> *we were only moving through the world together for a time*

The question marks the moment the poem turns from addressing an imagined listener or reader to a specified one, moving the poem from a general and unspecified time to a specific moment of the here and now. The poem, and by extension the speaker of the poem, and by extension the poet 'sees' the audience and their response, catching them out in a moment of possible judgement. If the poem is a confession, then maybe the audience is being asked to confess something as well.

In the poem, judgement is a foregone conclusion, indicated by the tiny three letter word 'yet' at the end of the line. The implication is that if you, the reader/listener, aren't being judgmental now, you will be eventually. The 'you' that is carrying out the judgment could be male or female, but the use of the word 'yet' betrays the speaker, who is also judging herself.

> *there was a double bassist who stood behind me*
> *and angled the body of his bass into mine*
> *and shadowed my hands on its neck*

In 'Age, Race, Class, and Sex' Audre Lorde draws on philosopher Paolo Freire to insist that 'the focus of revolutionary change is never merely the oppressive situations we seek to escape, but that piece of the oppressor which is planted deep within each of us and which knows only the oppressor's tactics, the oppressor's relationships'[25]. The oppressor inside the self is betrayed in this poem, in the body of the question, and the white space that surrounds the text.

and all I could feel
was heat from his skin

and the lightest breath
and even this might have been imagined

The 'yes' shouted out by the woman whose face I would not recognise on the street, but whose voice and accent I would know anywhere, could be called a heckle. It could also be called a joke. It could be called sexism. It could be called harm or harmful. It could be called judgemental. It could be called nothing. At the time I burst out laughing. It was funny. Part of me is still laughing, slightly hysterically.

Judith Butler argues that when a speaker utters a racist slur, it is harmful because of the history of that slur, because in the utterance of it, the speaker joins a 'linguistic community with a history of speakers'[26]. The idea that speaking an insult connects the speaker and the addressee to a linguistic community of racists who have uttered the same or similar racist insults is a powerful one and can be applied to all forms of bigoted speech, whether its motivations be sexism, ableism, homophobia, transphobia and on and on. In subsequent performances of this poem, I leave a beat of silence, of emptiness, in case another 'yes' is called out from the audience. I think it is true, that moment of judgment, that affirmative 'yes' is painful not because the addressee has judged, but because they have joined a community of people who have passed judgement on female desire.

I want to say to them now
        though all we are to each other is ghosts
once you were all that I thought of

Fast forward again to another event, another time. I am giving a seminar at a university. I read the poem and this time, I also tell the story of the 'yes'. A woman asks me what happens if someone shouts 'no'. At first I do not know what to answer. I realise that if someone shouted 'no', my own expectation of being judged reveals itself for what it is, which is my own sexism, which is that 'piece of the oppressor which is planted deep', which I carry with me, which I am writing out of myself, which I am both covering and uncovering with language, over and over again.

Another reading, this time in Manchester, in a basement bar. By this time, I am halfway through writing *All The Men I Never Married*[27], a collection made up of ex boyfriends and teachers, colleagues and strangers, men that I run with, men that I used to drink with, poets and musicians and scaffolders, men from a prison I worked in, men with whom I learned about desire and forgiveness, about violence and love.

when I whisper your names
it isn't a curse or a spell or a blessing

I read four of my *All The Men I Never Married* poems. I finish with No. 1, the list of men, the kickboxer, the trumpet players, the one, with an ear infection. I sell copies of my first collection, despite not reading anything from it. I am feeling pleased, as if the reading has been a success, as if something changed in the room after the poems entered that space. A man approaches, and at first I think he is there to buy a book. He tells me he has just started a Creative Writing MA and that he enjoyed the reading but found the poems were 'a bit catty'. As often happens in these situations, I don't know what to say. He says goodbye airily and leaves for his train.

At the time I am taken aback, but afterwards, I am already finding it funny. Imagine what he will do, I say to myself, when he reads the other forty poems! Part of me hugs myself in glee. I try to write a poem about him, but it doesn't work out.

A year ago, I would have been upset by this feedback. Now I find it interesting to examine what happens in my body, in my heart, in my mind when I hear words like 'catty' used to describe my work. I think about the word 'catty', how it would probably only ever be used to describe a woman. The Collins English dictionary tells me it means 'spiteful'. Synonyms include 'spiteful', 'mean', 'malicious' and 'malevolent'. The example that is given is 'His mother was catty, status-conscious and loud.' I cannot think of an equivalent word for a man. If a man was called 'catty', the implication would be that as well as being spiteful/mean/malicious/malevolent there would also be something inherently feminine in his behaviour.

It has taken a long time to work through my own desire for approval of my work, to reach for a place of exploration when met with disapproval. In *Talking Back, Thinking Black* bell hooks explores the desire for approval, explaining that this desire is not only naïve, but also dangerous, because 'such a longing can undermine radical commitment, compelling a change in voice so as to gain regard'[28]. To be able to sit with discomfort – both my own and the discomfort of the audience is always difficult. It is a journey that I will probably always be on as a poet. To understand that discomfort can lead to possible change for both myself and the audience. To realise that discomfort can lead to what bell hooks calls 'critical consciousness', which is not just naming and raising awareness of a personal experience of sexism, but 'critical understanding of the concrete material that lays the groundwork for that personal experience…and what must be done to transform it'[29].

I'm not mourning your passing or calling you here

At another reading, I leave the stage, and a man in his thirties approaches and compliments me first on my boots and then on my jumper. He says the shape of my jumper looks like I'm 'wearing a holster', that I look like 'I don't take any messing'. He does not mention anything about the reading, even though I have just finished, even though the words of my poems are still filling my mouth and my eyes. I think about the poet who told me 'You are so beautiful!' over and over. Compliment as a way of silencing, of deflecting, of minimizing.

I think about the gaze again, how men seem to find it so difficult to be looked at. I think about the female gaze in particular and how we can use it in poetry. At the Toronto International Film Festival in 2016 Joey Soloway defined the female gaze in three different ways. Firstly, as a way of 'feeling-seeing', which they describe as a way of getting inside a protagonist, and using the frame to 'share and evoke a feeling of being in feeling, rather than seeing.' Secondly, that the female gaze is a way of showing how it feels to be seen – what Soloway calls the 'gazed gaze'. Thirdly, that the female gaze returns the gaze, saying 'We see you, seeing us.'[30] Throughout the writing of *All the Men I Never Married*, I've experimented with these different ways of using the female gaze in poetry, but one of the things I found out was that even if I write with the female gaze, I cannot force the audience to see me, when what they want is to see woman not as poet, but as body, as gendered body. I can write about it later though – I can return the gaze, and say 'I saw you, seeing me.'

I smile and thank the man for his compliments about my boots and my jumper, and wonder about the type of messing I take, and am taking.

> *this is something harder*
> *like walking alone*
> *in the dusk and the leaves*

I read the poem again and again, in another town, another country, another season. Each time I read it, I risk reducing the men to objects, to paper-thin versions of fully rounded human beings. And yet. I hope they are rescued, I hope they are rescued by tenderness, by the act of placing them in a poem, the significance that brings. I hope the poem is rescued by the insertion of the perceiving self, who notices these men without grasping, without capturing. I hope to make the noticing full of moving on, full of letting go, full of refusing possession, of the man whose fingers flickered and danced when he talked, the man whose eyes were two pieces of winter sky. The perceiving of these details not to objectify, but as an attempt to describe what is between us with language, to hold with the female gaze both their bodies and their consciousness, both my body and my consciousness.

this is the naming of trees
this is a series of flames

I perform the poem again. I summon men into being with language, naming without naming, not wielding the gaze, which seems a violent action, but not looking away either. Each time I watch them all disappear, each time I honour the white space of the poem with silence, each time I ask the question, of you, of myself. I wait for a yes, or a no. I am resisting the oppressor within. I am also giving her a voice. I am also bringing her into the light.

this is watching you all disappear

If you would like to read 'Poems of Desire: A Mode of Attention' turn to page 114. If you would like to read about the shiftiness of sexism, turn to 'Sexism is a Slippery and Fluid Term' on page 76.

NOT LOOKING AWAY:
A POETICS OF ATTENTION

13.

Although we've only just met, he's already telling me
that no, my suitcase isn't heavy at all, as he lifts it
with one hand into the boot.

He's not even reached the end of the road
and he's already telling me I have a crazy soul,
that he can tell how crazy I am.

He asks me do I know what he means, and I smile
and pretend that I don't. He says all the women
he knows who are artists or poets or musicians are crazy.

Crazy, crazy, crazy he says and I wish I'd told him
I was an accountant instead but on he goes,
taking his eyes off the road

to tell me all women who are artists are crazy in bed,
do I know what he means, they want to try
crazy things in the bedroom.

If he stops the car I could open the door and run
or pull out my phone and pretend someone is calling
or ask him politely what's wrong.

I could laugh at the next thing he says while the voice
in my head whispers that somehow I've led him on,
that I was asking for it.

I remember a train journey, everyone crammed in
and a stranger's penis pressed against my leg,
convincing myself

I was imagining it, or he couldn't help it,
where else in the place could he put it?
When we pull up at the airport

my arm flings open the door before I give it permission,
my left leg finds the pavement before I can think.
Still I turn back to give him a tip

and he's laughing, saying relax, just relax, and I know
that he knows I'm afraid, that I've been afraid all my life,
but it's not this that makes me ashamed.

*If you think you have a problem with the male gaze, turn to page 48 (A Problem
with the Male Gaze). Otherwise, keep reading.*

7.

Imagine you're me, you're fifteen, the summer of '95,
and you're following your sister onto the log flume,
where you'll sit between the legs of a stranger.
At the bottom of the drop when you've screamed
and been splashed by the water, when you're about
to stand up, clamber out, the man behind
reaches forward, and with the back of his knuckle
brushes a drop of water from your thigh.

To be touched like that, for the first time.
And you are not innocent, you're fifteen,
something in you likes that you were chosen.
It feels like power, though you were only
the one who was touched, who was acted upon.
To realise that someone can touch you
without asking, without speaking, without knowing
your name. Without anybody seeing.

You pretend that nothing has happened,
you turn it to nothing, you learn that nothing
is necessary armour you must carry with you,
it was nothing, you must have imagined it.
To be touched – and your parents waiting at the exit
and smiling as you come out of the dark
and the moment being hardly worth telling.
What am I saying? You're fifteen and he is a man.

Imagine being him on that rare day of summer,
the bulge of car keys makes it difficult to sit
so he gives them to a bored attendant
who chucks them in a box marked PROPERTY.
A girl balanced in the boat with hair to her waist
and he's close enough to smell the cream
lifting in waves from her skin, her legs stretched out,
and why should he tell himself no, hold himself back?

He reaches forward, brushes her thigh with a knuckle,
then gets up to go, rocking the boat as he leaves.
You don't remember his face or his clothes,
just the drop of water, perfectly formed on your thigh,
before it's lifted up and away by his finger.
You remember this lesson your whole life,
that sliver/shiver of time, that moment in the sun.
What am I saying? Nothing. Nothing happened.

If you are wondering who I am talking to, turn to 'Mode of Address, or, Who Are You Talking To?' on page 56. Otherwise, keep reading.

4.

his dad handing out shots
        bright green
liquid sloshing
over the rim
        onto my wrist
steam on the kitchen windows
and the living room
        full of bodies
sitting in a circle
his mother nowhere
get em down
you Zulu warrior
        get em down
you Zulu chief chief chief
        follows me
the singing
        the dull thump of a bass
        the staircase bending
and swaying
        faraway bathroom
        my hand on the bannister
to keep myself here
        inside my body
        inside this house
        there's darkness to my left
there he is   on a bed
in the dark
        rolling a joint
        hey babe
I liked that word on his lips
        his friend
        at the open window
        letting smoke
slip out into the night

                it was good
to sit down

first I was there
           now I'm here
on the bed
      on my back
            a naked woman
blu-tacked and glossy
stares down from above

then the weight of him
           on top of me
at first it's funny
       as I try to get up
his knees   on my wrists
his hands   on my shoulders
that panic   in my belly
I'll remember it   as long as I live

the friend coming towards me
          a hand on my breast
the laughing   both of them laughing
my knee   into his groin

he topples sideways

and I'm up and out of the room
and into the night

and the dark asks why
      were you there in the dark
and the wind asks what
      were you doing upstairs
and the moon asks why
      were you wearing that skirt

but my body
        my body asks nothing
just whispers
                see
I did not let you down I did not
let you down I did not let you down

*Do you feel guilty for being a man? Turn to page 67 ('Guilty for Being a Man').
If not, keep reading.*

25.

When I tell them about my body
        and all the things it knows
they tell me about their guilt

they flourish their guilt
        as if they are matadors
in a city where people love blood

or they wave their guilt at me
        as if it is a flag of a newly formed country
and they are proud to be its citizens

sometimes they hold their guilt in their right hand
        and fan it out
like a deck of cards in a high-stakes game

or open up their guilt as if it is a book
        in a foreign language
they cannot understand

one held the two corners of his guilt
        as if it was a bedsheet
he must spread over my body

as if my body was a chair
        in a house closed up for the winter
and when he walked away

he left his guilt behind
        I run my hands along each edge
turns out his guilt is very small

not like a sheet at all
        more like a handkerchief

I shout have you forgotten something

but he is walking away whistling
       so I put it in my pocket
carry it with me always

If you are still unsure whether sexism exists, turn to 'Sexism is a Slippery and Fluid Term' on page 76.
If you would like to read about wilfulness, turn to 'An Electric Current: Poems of Wilfulness' on page 129.

A PROBLEM WITH THE MALE GAZE

After a reading, a man from the audience comes to tell me that my poem about a taxi driver ('All The Men I Never Married No. 13, page 39) shows that I have a problem with 'the male gaze'. I do not really know what he means. I haven't yet heard of the male gaze – I say something inane. I smile. I take it as a joke, though I know whatever he means, he does not mean it as a joke.

Later, I look up the male gaze, which leads me of course to Laura Mulvey and her ground-breaking essay 'Visual Pleasure and Narrative Cinema'. She examined the male gaze in relation to film theory, pointing out that on screen, women are represented as objects of male pleasure and subjected to a 'controlling and curious gaze'[31].

If I had known about Mulvey, would I have been able to say 'Yes, I do have a problem with the male gaze. Don't you?' Would I have been able to point out that the poem, in fact, is not about the male gaze anyway? If I had known about Mulvey, would my language still have failed me, as it has so many times before in moments like this?

Sara Ahmed in *Living A Feminist Life* wrote that '[w]hen you expose a problem, you pose a problem.'[32] In the inter-action between myself and the audience member, the taxi driver and his behaviour are no longer what's being scrutinized. Even the speaker's complicity in 'giving him a tip', in not verbally challenging him, even that is not what's under discussion. The whole complicated messiness of sexism and power are transformed into my 'problem with the male gaze', as if having a problem with the male gaze is a problem. I am accused of having a problem with the male gaze, as if this is something to be ashamed of, and at the time, I did not know how to defend myself.

I didn't know exactly what he meant, but I knew enough to imagine words like 'prude' and 'frigid' as he spoke, behind the words he actually said. I hadn't thought about these words since school, a whole lifetime and a world ago. Why did I think I could hear those words? Perhaps his tone of voice, the way he looked at me, the smile that I judged to be disdain, although I can't know this, because I did not ask him.

Now I do know what the male gaze is, it strikes me as such a strange thing to say to a woman, such a strange thing to be accused of. He was saying 'You have a problem with being regarded as an object!' And even so, and always, my first instinct is to hold up my hands in denial and say no, not me, not at all!

It is theory that I need in moments like this, so I can hold my nerve. A man says 'you clearly have a problem with the male gaze' and I move from subject and performer to object of the male gaze, an object which dares to have a problem with the way and manner it is looked at, except I know the poem is not about that, not about that at all.

The idea of using theory in everyday life, or of using everyday life to generate and consolidate theory or theoretical understandings is not a new one and can be traced back to Feminist Standpoint Epistemology, which began in the 1960s and 1970s as a way of using women's lived experiences to generate knowledge about wider society. A. T. Brooks says that as a methodology, it is a useful way of breaking down 'boundaries between academia and activism, between theory and practice'[33].

After this encounter with the man who (quite rightly) said I had a problem with the male gaze, I began to read about performative autoethnography. Although I didn't know it at the time, that night was the beginning of my understanding that these interactions would become an integral part of not just my research project and my PhD, but my own growth as a feminist, activist and poet, and finally, this book. It is not just the encounters, feedback and comments from audience members and readers which become part of this research and my writing, but also my own reaction to their reactions.

As Sara Ahmed points out 'becoming feminist is also about

generating ideas about the worlds we encounter'[34]. Generating ideas about experiences and encounters means I can survive being addressed like this. Ahmed writes that though these experiences can be wearing, they can also generate resources and energy. Once I started writing about them, I began to look forward to moments like this, writing the first sentence of an essay in my head before I leave the venue, sometimes, I'm ashamed to say, whilst the man concerned is still standing in front of me.

The female gaze, like the word sexism, is slippery and difficult to define. Alina Cohen, writing in *The Nation*, argues that '[o]n its own, the term is used to mean very little, amounting to a simplistic catchall for art made by women – reductive instead of empowering'[35], whilst Emily Nussbaum, in an article discussing the Amazon TV series *I Love Dick*, criticises the term's essentialism for implying that women 'can share one eye'[36].

If this is the only way this term can be used, then of course it is reductive, simplistic and essentialist. However, just as the 'male gaze' describes a way of looking, and began, as Alina Cohen points out, as a way to 'untether our minds and eyes from an aesthetic practice that supported the societal workings of patriarchy', then it follows that the female gaze is also a way of looking. Cohen argues that it should be defined as an 'aesthetic practice that supports the societal workings of universal equality'[37].

Utilizing the female gaze as an aesthetic practice in my own work involves looking without looking away, but also using the gaze to look at the relationality between people, and making this the focus of the gaze, rather than making the other the object. A. T. Brooks discusses the female gaze as a place where a 'double consciousness' can be articulated and shaped. This 'double consciousness' that she refers to is the consciousness I possess as a woman which is a 'heightened awareness not only of (their) own lives but of the lives of the dominant group (men) as well'[38].

It strikes me that there are further possibilities for this exploration of 'double consciousness' and the female gaze. Other minority groups must also experience this 'double consciousness' in different ways. How does this binary of the male and female gaze work in terms of the way that they write poetry?

In Joey Soloway's lecture at the 2016 Toronto International Film Festival, they described the female gaze as a 'socio-political justice-demanding way of seeing', a way of 'privileging the body and emotion' and of 'returning the gaze, not just in the act of looking back, but to say "I see you seeing me".'[39]

How we can wield this gaze in poetry, and what it might mean to do this is a question I keep circling around. I think about Virginia Woolf, who wrote in *A Room of One's Own* that '[w]omen have served all these centuries as looking-glasses possessing the magic and delicious power of reflecting the figure of man at twice its natural size.'[40] How can I use the female gaze in poetry, how can I look at men without simply reversing this position, turning them into looking-glasses?

We have so many words for different ways of looking – to gaze, watch, see, glance, peruse, stare, observe, study, examine, regard, scan, gawk, glare, scrutinize, consider, peek, peep, ogle and survey. The word 'look' seems to be full of movement and implies not just the act of looking, but the act of looking away. The choice to 'look' at experiences of sexism has resulted in an experiential poetics in which men and masculinity are examined as a way of reflecting on gendered experience.

Rosemarie Waldrop writes that '[w]e come to know anything that has any complexity by glimpses. So it is best to have as many different glimpses from as many different perspectives as possible, rather than trying to develop a linear argument where one follows from another'[41]. I decide to develop a methodology of the glimpse throughout this book. How else to consider versions and variations of masculinity and the different ways that sexism plays out in a woman's life? The methodology of the glimpse would involve the act of placing these acts of sexism, these versions and variations of masculinity into a poem – one way of wielding the female gaze.

To return to Joey Soloway again – poetry about sexism says 'I see you seeing me.' It privileges the body and emotion. It is a way of 'feeling-seeing.' Looking at sexism often causes it to change shape, to shift, to move, even to become revealed in the room when previously it was hidden. Poetry steps into the space created by the shiftiness of sexism and forces us to look closer, look harder, at what we may have told ourselves was nothing. Often stories of sexism, particularly everyday sexism have an absence at their centre. This idea of 'nothing' is what I return to again and again in my creative and critical work. The word 'nothing' becomes an effective protection, a wall to stop the mind imagining not only what could have happened, but also what the world might look like if these things did not keep happening.

In 'All the Men I Never Married No. 7' (page 41) one of the things I wanted to explore was the idea of nothingness which is often at the heart of encounters with sexism. Nothingness is a tool of the perpetrator to minimise both their conduct and any possible effects of their conduct. It's also a coping strategy of the victim, often used to minimise the impact of a perpetrator's conduct on the victim's sense of self and feelings of safety as they move through the world. In this poem, a man touches a girl's thigh on a fairground ride. The speaker of the poem says

> You pretend that nothing has happened,
> you turn it to nothing, you learn that nothing
> is necessary armour you must carry with you,
> it was nothing, you must have imagined it.

Often in poetry, the pronoun 'you' is built on shifting sands and can mean both the self, and / or the 'you' who is reading or listening to the poem, or a 'you' that the poem is about. However, I wanted to make clear that the audience or reader are being directly addressed, right from the first line: 'Imagine you're me', asking them to put themselves inside the experience, inside the body of a fifteen-year-old girl.

This is a deliberate technique to try to activate the female gaze as defined by Joey Soloway, a 'conscious effort to create empathy as a political tool'. Soloway goes on to say that the female gaze is also a way of drawing attention to 'the way the world feels for women when they move their bodies through the world.'[42]

I also wanted to experiment and see if I could switch between the female gaze and the male gaze. In stanza 4, I address the audience again, but this time invite them to imagine themselves as the man seeing the girl:

> *A girl balanced in the boat with hair to her waist*
> *and he's close enough to smell the cream*
> *lifting in waves from her skin, her legs stretched out*

I find myself increasingly uncomfortable when I read these lines during a performance and this discomfort has grown from a tiny needle-like question to feeling as if my skin is crawling when I say the words, although on the surface of it they might seem fairly innocuous. Part of my discomfort stems from wondering whether the shift between one gaze and the other translates to the audience, or have we as a society become so used to the gaze that objectifies that it feels if not normal, then so commonplace as to not be worthy of notice?

In the final stanza, I return again to the female gaze. Every time I read this poem, I am left feeling as if I am on a giant swing, my head being turned this way and that, between the female gaze and the male gaze, between one world and the other, between two ways of thinking that feel so disparate that placing them in the same poem has created something inherently unstable, something radical.

In a review of the 1995 novel *In the Cut* by Susanna Moore, Katherine Angel writes that seeing sexual assault as 'exceptional, as a feverish conflagration, invites excitement about it – enables, perhaps, its eroticisation'[43]. Throughout the collection *All the Men I Never Married,* my aim was to explore the many different forms of sexism in order to expose the day-to-day grind and the monotony of women's daily contact with it, to examine rather than fetishize these experiences and to show how they are not isolated events but all part of a continuum.

Angel's article also explores how violence and desire are simultaneously two opposing but interconnected forces. She asks 'How are we to represent in writing, the fact that sexual desire lives entangled with sexual violence? How are we to deal, in art, with the powerful, destabilizing forces of both violence and desire?'[44]

The problem explored in this poem, or one of the problems explored here are that those two opposing forces of violence and desire are so unstable as to be almost unrecognisable. The revelation in the poem that the girl enjoys 'being the one chosen, who was acted upon' is troubling. It troubled me when I wrote it, when I remembered this feeling.

This first experience of being desired is tangled irretrievably for me with the violation of unpermitted touching, and it's taken a lifetime to understand that violation is always a form of violence. At the time, I didn't understand what had happened. When I started writing the poem, I didn't understand what had happened. Desire, violence and sexism overlap and intersect and our bodies understand before we do. Was it complicity in that moment, to be fifteen and 'like that I was chosen?' In that moment, I felt powerful, as if my body had taken control of anothers and compelled them to act. I was too young to understand the shifting sands that kind of power is built upon. I could feel those two 'powerful, destabilizing forces' that Angel talks about at work, but I did not have the language to speak their names.

Have you ever seen a man move through a crowd, and touch the lower back of a woman to move her out of his way, or perhaps rest his hand on her shoulder? I have been the one touched in this way so many times, but I have never seen a man do it to other men to pass by. If it happened to me now, I'd feel annoyed. Perhaps I'd shrug that hand off, or move away or say 'Excuse me' sharply. I'd feel it as an intrusion, a violation. But back in my twenties, when to be desired felt like a kind of power – back then, I would have turned and smiled as I moved out of the way.

To continue reading 'Not Looking Away: A Poetics of Attention' turn to page 39.

MODE OF ADDRESS, OR, WHO ARE YOU TALKING TO?

In a conversation with my husband about his work as a therapist, we talked about how he uses confrontation in a therapeutic setting. He said that rather than viewing confrontation as an attack or something aggressive, instead he sees it as a way of challenging set patterns of behaviour by coming alongside the client and working with them. This reframing and new way of thinking about a word that felt familiar, a word I thought I understood had a lasting impact on me. The root of the word 'confront' fits with my husband's sense of the word. 'Con' means 'together, with', whilst 'front' comes from 'forehead, brow.' I think of the word 'together', the word 'heads.' Together, heads. Heads, together.

In an academic paper discussing relational learning, Mark Murphy and Tom Brown argue that in a higher educational setting, students must be 'disturbed or transformed'[45] to be successful. Should great art, great poetry also disturb or transform us, should it confront us in some way – not for the sake of educating, but to discover something about ourselves and our place in the world?

Claudia Rankine's 2015 collection *Citizen* is a book I've returned to again and again, both throughout the time when I was researching for my PhD, but also afterwards. It's a book that changed my life. It did disturb and transform me, in the way that I think the greatest poetry always does. I also felt confronted – both in my old understanding of it, but also in the way that my husband reframed the word.

This new sense of the word 'confront' seems to fit with Claudia Rankine's philosophy around talking about race. Her 2020 book *Just Us: An American Conversation*[46] sets out to explore how black and white people can talk to each other about white supremacy. Diep Tran, writing on the website 'Andscape' points out that Rankine sees herself as 'something of an anthropologist looking for clues on how to overcome

America's racial chasm.'[47] This idea of a poet working in this way is exciting – poetry as intrinsically woven into society, but poetry also as a way of finding something out, of discovering, of learning.

The poet and academic Mary Jean Chan writes that Rankine has created a 'poetics of racial trauma' allowing for 'complex subjectivity and intimate address'[48]. One of the primary techniques that Rankine uses to achieve this is her use of the second person pronoun 'you'. The shiftiness of this pronoun opens up the possibilities of address in her work. The addressee could be the poet herself, the speaker in the poem, but also the reader of the text.

The use of 'you' often makes the reader feel as if they are being directly addressed, almost as if they are being told a story of their life: 'You are in the dark, in the car, watching the black-tarred street being swallowed by speed;'[49]. This is intimate lyric writing at its best – its apparent peacefulness troubled by the use of 'black-tarred' which called into my mind 'tar and feathering' – used notoriously by the Ku Klux Klan.

The sentence turns on the hinge of the semi-colon, after the black-tarred street is 'swallowed by speed;' Rankine then writes 'he tells you his dean is making him hire a person of color when there are so many great writers out there.'[50] When I first wrote this essay, over two years ago, I wrote that a white reader is 'jolted' out of thinking they can inhabit the 'you' because of the words spoken here. I was comfortably inhabiting the 'you', but then I was shocked out of this cosy assumption.

After reading Rankine's work, I cannot inhabit the 'you' without thinking about what that means. If I am the 'you' who is addressed, it means the person doing the addressing, the person being so casually racist and offensive, assumes I share this feeling with them, that I may even sympathise with them. My first instinct is to recoil. I cannot be the 'you.' But of course I can be, and what it means to be the 'you' as a white person is a completely different experience to what it might feel to be a black person reading Rankine's work. As a white person, I read it and feel shocked and then immediately want to pull myself away from the text, a kneejerk reaction to 'prove' that this type of thinking is nothing to do with me! Later, I feel angry that people who say things like this are in positions of power, and embarrassed that reading about racism can still shock me, proof of the privilege that I live with each day as a white person.

This feels like the female gaze in action. I think back again to Joey Soloway's 2016 definition of the female gaze as a 'conscious effort to create empathy as a political tool'[51]. Mary Jean Chan writes that Claudia Rankine uses spectatorship and positionality 'as a means of bearing intimate witness to racial injustice' and as a way of cultivating 'empathy towards others[52] which fits perfectly with Soloway's defined aims of the female gaze.

In the last part of this section, Rankine outlines what it means to have these words (and words like them) spoken. She talks about the medical term 'John Henryism' – which refers to 'people exposed to stresses stemming from racism. They achieve themselves to death trying to dodge the buildup of erasure.'[53] This difference in how language and the world is experienced is a focus throughout *Citizen,* not just in terms of race, but also gender and class as well. This is a text that asks white readers to see themselves as racialised and to take notice of the way they move through the world within that race.

There is also a great response to comments like this folded within Rankine's work as well. The third paragraph starts 'Why do you feel comfortable saying this to me?'[54] – but it's not clear whether the speaker says this out loud, or only thinks it. I file that away as a response I can use in future if someone says something racist, sexist, homophobic, transphobic. A response I can use when language fails. A response I can use without erasing or speaking for black people, that shows that I don't agree with the slur being spoken. A response that puts the onus back on the speaker to explain themselves.

Danez Smith's collection *Homie*, published in 2020, takes on the problem of the 'white gaze' by not addressing white people at all. In a recent interview in *The Guardian*, Smith said:

> With *Homie* I stopped asking myself: 'What should I do with the white gaze?' Because I realised I wasn't interested in it. I asked myself: 'Why am I spending so much time worried about this gaze? I think white people can learn a lot from the poems, but that's not who I'm writing for.[55]

Smith sets out their stall from the outset of *Homie* by providing two titles to the collection, one for use by white people, one for non-white people. This gesture is political, playful and confrontational. It extends and pushes at the mode of address enacted by lyric poetry, and any stereotypical notions of its traditional readership. In my own work, I have struggled and wrestled with thoughts of who I am addressing. Unlike Smith, I haven't managed to get to the point of being disinterested in the male gaze. I still want men to read my work, to come to readings, to listen. I want them to be confronted, to be disturbed, maybe even to be transformed.

Despite this, I've noticed myself getting irritated in question and answer sessions with mixed audiences. Most of the time, it's men who speak first, that share their experience, that express contrition, guilt (see 'Guilty for Being A Man', page 67). Sometimes I think in the rush to speak, many men don't stop to think or listen, and it begins to feel like another form of oppression.

I was recently invited to read from my second collection *All the Men I Never Married*, and after I finished my reading, the male host began to speak. He shared his own experience of being at a single sex school, and the sexist behaviours and language he'd witnessed, concluding with the opinion that single sex schools are (and were) a bad idea. The positive and negative attributes of single sex schools are obviously a deeply complex subject, and there is not space here to go into this in detail and do it justice, but his leap to the conclusion that boys learn to behave better if girls are present fascinated me. It seemed reasonable to him that ensuring boys behave well should be just another part of a girl's curriculum, an extra emotional, physical and spiritual labour that girls and women should undertake. He hadn't thought to question his own assumptions – that boys couldn't possibly learn not to be sexist from other men and each other – which of course diminishes men and boys as well.

The tendency to make women responsible for the behaviour of men, and consequently blame them when men behave badly is not a new story, but rather a recurring trope that is embedded in the stories we tell ourselves and that are told about women. In the Bible, Eve is a temptress who lures Adam to commit the sin of eating the apple in the Garden of Eden, and there are other women who bring about the downfall of otherwise upstanding men – Salome, Delilah, Jezebel.

In our contemporary culture, we see it in the tendency towards victim-blaming, which ranges from rape victims being described in the media with extraneous details such as what they were wearing (short skirts) or what they were doing (drinking) being contributing factors to their rape, as if there is no active agent doing the raping. In a condescending social media post from the Nottingham Police, women were advised that 'Women who walk alone especially at night are at risk of harassment, or even physical assault. It is always best to walk with someone, or in an area where there are other people.'[56] The backlash from this post meant it was quickly deleted, but it is an interesting example of the way that many people still believe that the way to stop violence against women is to limit the freedoms of women, not to change the behaviour of men.

It was the experience at the reading with the man who shared his opinion on single sex schools that led me to reflect again on the Danez Smith quote, and how my position feels as if it is changing, even as I write this essay. I think I am now moving much closer to Danez Smith's approach – although I still can't write this or say it without feeling my own form of guilt. So much of my work explores my own complicity with sexism, or at least examines what may look like complicity on the surface – and it is women I want to hear from when I am talking about complicity, which is another name for surviving, or coping with this world.

It's taken years for that part of me that wants to please, to be complicit and agreeable, to talk about sexism with a smile on my face, to not sound like I'm just 'going on', to feel safe enough to rest. She's done her work, she's got me this far. Now there's another woman rising inside me.

I think of Sylvia Plath's 'Mirror', where the mirror tells us 'In me she has drowned a young girl, and in me an old woman / Rises towards her day after day, like a terrible fish.'[57] I've always thought it is the woman in the poem whose horror of aging we feel, but in fact, it's the mirror speaking, and the mirror's gaze. At first I thought this articulation of the mirror's horror of aging was Plath writing with the traditional 'male gaze' and repeating stereotypes about older women. Now I think there is something more complex going on. That 'terrible fish' is rising towards us, looking back at us. Now I think of the female gaze, the 'I see you seeing me gaze' every time I read this poem.

In Denise Levertov's poem 'In Mind' there is a 'woman / of innocence' who is 'kind and very clean without / ostentation.' Levertov finishes the description of this woman 'but she has / no imagination.' The poem contrasts this woman with a 'turbulent moon-ridden girl / or old woman, or both' who 'knows strange songs' and finishes the description and the poem with 'but she is not kind.'[59] We know from the title that all these versions of womanhood exist in the mind of the speaker. I felt so excited when I read this poem by the possibilities it contained – that these different variations of womanhood or girl hood could exist inside the mind, to be called up or revealed when needed, and that a figure of womanhood could exist without being kind, that the point of her existence was to sing strange songs and wear 'opals and rags'. Levertov's 'moon-ridden girl' would have no interest in being complicit, in being agreeable.

I make a promise to myself, to be more turbulent, to be more moon-ridden, to sing stranger songs, to rise towards myself like a terrible fish, to always be looking back, even when I am the looked upon.

★

In 'A Woman Speaks' Audre Lorde challenges the tendency to assume that women in poems are white, that women are white. The woman speaking in Lorde's poem is a generic woman who seems to be speaking on behalf of women in general: 'I do not dwell / within my birth nor my divinities / who am ageless and half-grown' before the poem finishes with the lines 'I / am woman / and not white.'[59] Lorde pulls the rug out from underneath the complacent white reader – the surprise of these last three lines forces me to confront my own surprise and to examine my assumptions about who the speaker is in this poem.

In *Gendering Poetry,* published in 2003, Vicki Bertram argues that 'There are few modes of public discourse in which women can speak as *women,* and this is reflected in their poetry, where it is rare to find an explicit address to other women, a collective female discourse.'[60] Whilst I agree with Bertram that it is difficult to speak as a woman, and this is true for many reasons, she fails to acknowledge that female poets such as Audre Lorde and Claudia Rankine have been con-sistently speaking as women (more specifically black women) in their poetry. Who they are addressing, however, is much more complex.

Rankine is intentional about her use of positionality throughout *Citizen,* a genre-bending book, containing prose poems, short essays, photographs and art. On one page, we encounter a photograph that depicts a crowd of white people, some looking towards the camera, others looking upwards towards a tree. The photograph is of a public lynching, and in the original version two black bodies hang from a tree. In this version, what we see are only the faces of the white men, women and children, fixed forever in expressions of excitement, happiness and even triumph. In Rankine's version of the photograph, the black bodies are missing. We see only the white bodies. We are aware that these white bodies can be described in various ways. Some are participants. Are all of them participants, even the witnesses, even the spectators? As readers we are also participants in this. We look at the photograph again. Perhaps we google it to see the full, unedited horror. We become spectators, looking at what is happening, and we are witnesses to trauma, although at least in Rankine's version, the traumatised bodies are no longer the spectacle. What we are left witnessing instead is violence, which resides in the white bodies who carried out or watched the act of violence, rather than in the bodies who were acted upon. In our passivity, we also become active participants, because looking is never truly passive. We are implicated by our looking.

Rankine's erasure of the victims in this photograph means we cannot be spectators to black trauma. Instead, we are left looking at the people who took part, either by participating, witnessing or spectating, and they are looking back at us. *Citizen* is full of moments like this, where the black female gaze is activated to shift the reader between these positions of spectator, witness and participant, creating empathy, but also returning the gaze.

This idea of black bodies and the violence carried out on them being used as a spectacle was highlighted in 2017 at the Whitney Biennial Gallery when the white artist Dana Schutz exhibited 'Open Casket', a painting inspired by the life and story of Emmett Till, whose murder at 15 years of age was one of the sparks that ignited the civil rights movement. The work was criticised by activists in an open letter, whilst another activist staged a protest, standing in front of the painting to block anyone viewing it whilst wearing a shirt reading 'Black Death Spectacle'.

Rankine discusses the visibility or invisibility of black people in episodes throughout *Citizen*. Incident after incident is recounted where black people are not seen or made invisible. A white friend calls the speaker of the poem – the 'you' – by the name of a black housekeeper. A nun doesn't notice a white girl cheating. A white man at a checkout pushes in front of the 'you' and says 'Oh my God, I didn't see you... No, no, no, I really didn't see you.'[61]

In an interview in *Bomb* magazine Rankine said:

> I am not interested in narrative, or truth, or truth to power, on a certain level; I am fascinated by affect, by positioning, and by intimacy...what happens when I stand close to you? What is your body going to do? What's my body going to do? On myriad levels, we are both going to fail, fail, fail each other and ourselves. The simplicity of the language is never to suggest truth, but to make transparent the failure.[62]

Sara Ahmed describes the mapping of a series of seemingly minor incidents of racism or sexism as a 'biography of violence'[63], arguing that this then creates evidence of a structure, or a series of events, or a pattern. As Mary Jean Chan writes, Rankine's depiction of relational failures and her 'intimate witnessing'[64] of them invites us to be intimate too, invites us into the position of witnesses, along with all the responsibilities that position holds.

This idea of making relational failure transparent is something I'm also interested in exploring in my own work. It's implicit in the title of my second collection: *All the Men I Never Married*. The title is both ironic and serious in its setting out of one way men and women relate to each other, as if this is the only way of relating. My poetry examines this idea of relational failure, as opposed to a 'truth' about how men or women behave. Part of this relational failure is the failure of language – in many of the poems, the speaker of the poem fails to speak out for different reasons, or conversely, hides their true feelings with language.

Examples of this relational failure which also becomes a failure of language can be found throughout *All the Men I Never Married*. In 'All the Men I Never Married No. 8' (page 163) the speaker is coerced into a conversation with a stranger instead of doing what she wants to do, which is read. In 'All the Men I Never Married No. 13' (page 39) the speaker is silent and hides the fear she really feels in a multitude of ways – by smiling, by giving a tip, by pretending nothing is wrong. In 'All the Men I Never Married No. 12' (page 101) the speaker does not even finish a sentence before being interrupted.

Like Rankine, I wanted to use relational failure to examine experiences of microaggression and trauma to create my own 'biography of violence'. However, whilst Rankine's main focus was everyday moments of racism (although she also writes intersectionally about sexism as well, focusing particularly in *Citizen* on the treatment of the tennis player Serena Williams) my focus was to explore experiences of sexism and female desire.

Following Rankine's example, I have experimented with the positioning of the reader or audience member as both participant, spectator and witness in different poems, and how shifting this positioning in the course of a poem can produce different effects. In 'All the Men I Never Married No. 7' (page 41) I ask the audience to 'Imagine you're me' at the beginning of the poem, positioning them as participants, and by the end of the poem, I ask them to 'imagine you're him', inviting them to change position and be a participant, the one 'doing' rather than the one being 'done to'.

White space gives this moment in 'All the Men I Never Married No. 7' importance, to make it not-nothing, to say nothing terrible happened, but at the same time, *something* terrible happened. The use of the direct address means I can also bear intimate witness as well as inviting the audience to do the same, using the female gaze to, as Soloway put it, 'create empathy as a political tool'.

To continue reading 'Not Looking Away: A Poetics of Attention', turn to page 43.

GUILTY FOR BEING A MAN

Two men I know, on two different occasions after I have finished performing, tell me my poetry makes them feel 'guilty for being a man'. This is not the first time a man has said these words to me, but it is the first time it has happened twice in the same week. I tell both men I do not want them to feel guilty. I express regret and worry that they feel guilty. At the same time, deep down where they cannot see and I can hardly feel it, I am angry. I am irritated, and I'm impatient, but I don't give voice to any of it at the time.

Later, I start to reflect on this feeling of guilt that those men came to me to talk about. I stumble across a quote by Audre Lorde:

> I cannot hide my anger to spare your guilt, nor hurt feelings, nor answering anger, for to do so insults and trivialises all our efforts. Guilt is not a response to anger; it is a response to one's own actions or lack of action. If it leads to change it can be useful, since it is then no longer guilt but the beginning of knowledge.[65]

When I read this quote, I feel as if a light has shone on to my experience, on to my feelings. I understand where my anger came from. Later on, I experience my own guilt, when I realise that I almost used this quote out of context, without acknowledging that Lorde was addressing a feminist conference, and more specifically, white feminists' failure to listen, hear and understand black feminists' concerns.

I am at the 2017 Forward Prize ceremony. Claudia Rankine stands up to read from her shortlisted collection *Citizen*. I start to feel more and more uncomfortable. It is the first time I start to really understand my own complicity in racism, that I unconsciously participate in racist structures. Her recounting of everyday racism and articulation of white privilege leaves me feeling guilty and ashamed. I do not, however, go and tell

Claudia Rankine this. I vow to do better. I can see changes that I can make in the way I programme events, in my reading and in my research.

I start to think about how recounting experiences of sexism might have a similar impact on both men and women – could writing experiential poetry about sexism bring sexism to the consciousness of men and women in a similar way?

I realise I am drawing an analogy between my behaviour as a white woman when confronted about racism in society and the behaviour of men when confronted about sexism, and that in doing this, I am moving on from considering racism and focusing again on my own situation. In their 1991 article 'Obscuring the Importance of Race: The Implication of Making Comparisons Between Racism and Sexism (and Other-Isms)' Grillo and Wildman explain that 'The use of analogies provides both the key to greater comprehension and the danger of false understanding.'[66] Perhaps the secret to greater comprehension is not to rush to analogy, but instead to sit with those moments of discomfort for a while longer before moving onward.

A man says "Your poetry makes me feel guilty for being a man" and I try to understand my anger at this response, although by now, it does not quite feel like anger. I am trying to understand my own feelings, underneath/covered by anger, by impatience. Maybe underneath my anger is guilt, a direct response to their guilt. I have made them 'feel guilty for being a man' and I in turn feel guilty, because after all, they have done none of the things to me that I am complaining of. Guilt is passed back and forth between the two of us.

Guilt is an emotion of social control and has been used as a form of punishment, probably since punishment was invented. When men admit feelings of guilt for behaviour they have not carried out, the conversation changes from being about an experience of sexism, to being about their feelings of guilt, and how just or unjust they are. An admission of guilt can be a way of closing the conversation down, a way of making it seem as if men are being punished, just because a woman is talking about her experience of sexism. As Sara Ahmed writes in *Living a Feminist Life* 'You can cause unhappiness by noticing something.'[67] I would argue it's also possible to cause guilt by noticing something and then daring to name it.

Strange things happen to some men when they feel they are being looked at. In the *Phenomenology of Perception* Maurice Merleau-Ponty writes that:

> Man does not ordinarily show his body, and, when he does, it is either nervously or with the intention to fascinate. It seems to him that the alien gaze that glances over his body steals it from him, or, on the contrary, that the exhibition of his body will disarm and deliver the other person up to him...[68]

Reading this made me wonder if this is what is at the heart of some of the defensive reactions that have come from some men towards the poems in *All the Men I Never Married*, that men are just not accustomed to being looked at.

All the Men I Never Married invites the reader to look at men, but it is not their bodies that are displayed. I am looking at a man and placing him inside a poem, not to 'steal' his body, or to allow the display of his body to 'disarm' or 'deliver' him, or to reduce his body to passivity and render mine an active agent, or vice versa, or even to make him feel guilty. My intention is always to examine what Luce Irigaray in *To Be Two* calls the 'between-us'[69], in her attempt to define a possible relationship between two people that differs from a subject-object relationship and instead is about recognising and respecting the interiority and alterity of the other. This path between the self and another and what it might look like, and what might happen in this space, is fertile ground for poetry.

In writing about the 'between-us', the path between the

'between-us' is both the path between the speaker and the men in the poems, and the path between writer and reader, and between myself and the text. Merleau-Ponty writes, 'Thus, I can see one object insofar as objects form a system or a world, and insofar as each of them arranges the others around itself like spectators of its hidden aspects...'[70]. By writing about one man, maybe all the others are called to arrange themselves around the first, 'spectators of its hidden aspects' that are now not so hidden, not so secret. Is this where that troubling guilt comes from?

To continue reading 'Not Looking Away: A Poetics of Attention' turn to page 46.

BETWEEN US: A POETICS OF PERCEPTION

10.

two hours with you   sitting at opposite ends
of your single bed

living the dream you say
        I can't tell if this is sarcasm

your feet level   with my chest
my feet level   with your waist

       almost like   being a teenager again
       almost like   a giving in

you put your hand on my ankle
        your eyes are closed

a train passes   the room shudders

the only thing speaking is your hand
        the slow circle of your thumb

I can't tell if you're dreaming
        or if this is something else

do we all have an ex we can't forget
not the one   that got away

but the one who left
not the one   who left for good

but the one that stays just out of reach
your thumb relearning the bone of my ankle

I know your patterns
             I know how this goes

maybe we have nothing left
         to talk about any more

can you feel my body humming
         underneath your fingers

do we all have someone   we can't forgive?

22.

That night, which I knew would be the last night,
when I said *be straight with me* and you kissed me again,
when I said *I think I'm more into this than you are*
and you kissed me again and said *let's go back to bed.*
Afterwards I said *answer me*, the night and the morning
still lodged in my chest, my body turning under your hands
as you said *yes, I guess you probably are* and then I knew
I could not fall into the body place with you again.
That the body can want one thing and the heart another,
that the heart can already be moving on
while the body yearns for the familiar embrace once again.
These were the things I learnt from your face,
tracing the outline of your bones and the slickness
of your chest. In the day you put on a suit and tie
and caught a train to another place. I ran with you
in the wind and rain, on the track or at the beach
and we thought nobody knew we went home together.
You did your washing on a Sunday and folded your clothes
and ironed your shirts and nothing could change this routine.
You were full of ambition for yourself and disdain
for your students. But in the dark you were none of this,
you were heat and blood and fingers and chest,
there was nothing neat about you.
Where are you now, did you get to London like you wanted,
are you in another immaculate flat, do you still read the papers
at the weekend, is everything tucked in, put away?
Part of me still hovers there, trying to work out
how you managed it, to hold something back,
how I managed it.

36.

he did not come to me as a swan
          or a shower of gold

                    he was never a white bull
          the sort to lure you away from home

he was just a man
          like and unlike any other

                    he stood by my bed in the dark
                              afterwards no wife turned up
to take revenge
          to transform me into a cow

no god or father scooped me up
          the way Apollo carried Paris

from the battlefield
(there was no battlefield)

I didn't know it would be me
          who carried him here

                    didn't know about walking
                              the length of the self

                    how the self disappears
                              how hard it would be

                              after five ten fifteen years

If you are interested in relationality, turn to 'Something in the Telling: A Poetics of Relationality' on page 84.

If your body has ever spoken without you knowing what it said, turn to 'The Body is the Blindspot of Speech' on page 145.

If you would like to read 'What Is Between-Us' turn to page 158.

SEXISM IS A SLIPPERY AND FLUID TERM

In 2014, Laura Bates set up the 'Everyday Sexism' website. Women were invited to upload their experiences – from the 'niggling and normalized to the outrageously offensive'[71]. In April 2015, twenty months after the project was launched, there were 100,000 entries on the website. In her book *Everyday Sexism* which followed the project, Bates writes that while she 'initially set out to record daily instances of sexism' it quickly 'came to document cases of serious harassment and assault, abuse and rape.'[72] Adrienne Rich wrote that when a woman tells the truth she creates 'the possibility for more truth around her'[73] and this can be seen in action, both on the Everyday Sexism website and today across various social media sites.

In 2017, the celebrity Alyssa Mirano spoke out on Twitter about her experience of sexual assault, encouraging followers to reply with 'Me Too' if they had experienced something similar. The #MeToo went viral as women spoke out about their experiences of gender-based violence. It's important to note that whilst this was the moment the #MeToo arrived into wider public consciousness, it was actually conceived ten years prior by the activist Tarana Burke as part of a grass-roots movement aimed at helping black women who were survivors of sexual assault and violence.

What was apparent from the range of stories shared in both campaigns was that the term 'sexism' often becomes a catch-all term for different extremes of behaviour. 'Sexism' in itself is a slippery and fluid term which resists definition and boundaries to encompass harassment, oppression, abuse and assault. There still seems to be a lack of understanding from some people about the links between individual experiences of sexism and how that is shaped and defined by wider societal constructs.

Rosalind Gill, writing in 2011 called for a reconceptualization of sexism as an 'agile, dynamic, changing and diverse set of malleable representations and practices of power.'[65] Even the term 'Everyday Sexism' with its connotation of being casual or ordinary comes under pressure when the 'everyday' is more serious and more violent than has been previously acknowledged.

In the same way that the Everyday Sexism website was inundated with serious accounts of sexual harassment and assault alongside more minor incidents, I realised that in my own work I was using the blanket label of sexism to cover the many types of gender-based harassment and aggression that I had experienced, when a more accurate description for these incidents would be assault. The word 'sexism' had become a coping mechanism for me, a way of diminishing or minimising concrete lived experience.

The act of putting the white space of a poem around a recounting of an experience of sexism allowed me to look at the experience differently. Gregory Orr in *Poetry As Survival* argues that the act of writing a lyric poem means we have 'shifted the crisis to a bearable distance from us; removed it to the symbolic but vivid world of language. Second, we have actively *made* and shaped this model of our situation rather than passively endured it as lived experience.'[66] Shaping a model of my situation, as Orr puts it, allowed me to 'see' my own experiences of sexism differently, in that it enabled me to understand both my own complicity and the true weight of these experiences.

Translating a lived experience of sexism, or in the case (of my first book, domestic violence) did shift it to what Orr calls a 'bearable distance'. Each experience feels contained by the structure of the poem. However, it also led me to realise that writing as an act in itself is messy work, and perhaps doubly so when writing about sexism and gender-based violence. Sara Ahmed uses the phrase 'messy work' about diversity work, and points out that a writer has to 'think strategically, we also have to accept our complicity, we forego any illusions of parity; we give up the safety of exteriority'[76]. The paradox of writing producing both a 'bearable distance' and asking us to 'give up the safety of exteriority' is not lost on me. I believe both things can be true, even at the same time.

This messiness is complicated further during performances. At a reading, sexism sometimes appears in the room whilst I read about sexism, or I am subjected to sexism in conversations afterwards. Negotiating these conversations, learning to confront both myself and others without leaping to defensiveness, to listen without feeling attacked is a messy, ongoing life's work.

In *Writing Otherwise: Experiments in Cultural Criticism,* J. Wolff and J. Stacey write that 'feminine existence is in fact a traumatised existence'[77]. These words made it possible to reframe some of the things that I'd experienced, and my reaction to them.

L.S. Brown's essay 'Not Outside the Range' argues that to understand that women's existence is traumatised may require a reframing and expansion of our understanding of trauma (and resultant post-traumatic stress disorder) to encompass the 'everyday assaults on integrity and personal safety'[78]. The traditional definition of PTSD, according to the *Diagnostic and Statistical Manual of Mental Disorders* required the individual to have been confronted with death, threatened death, or actual threatened injury or violence, including sexual violence. It is only very recently that sexual violence was included in this definition at all.

The historical recognition of PTSD, has, according to Brown, always been limited to 'public and male experiences of trauma' and has failed to acknowledge the daily lived experiences of women and other minority groups. Maria Root coined the term 'insidious trauma' – a term used to describe 'the effects of oppression that are not necessarily overtly violent or threatening to bodily well-being at the given moment but that do violence to the soul and spirit.'[79]

At a recent event with a fellow poet, M, who happens to be trans, I couldn't help but think about this idea of 'insidious trauma'. I introduced M to another poet, who I'll call B. We started to talk about M's new work, which I was excited to hear more about. M said she felt as if she was really breaking new ground with this new work, but then paused and turned to B and explained that she was trans and was writing about it in poetry for the first time.

We continued to talk about poetry, and poetic techniques. There was nothing unsupportive or negative about B's reaction. B continued to be interested, and friendly. And yet, it felt to me like an inherently violent thing, to be talking about poetry one minute, and then for M to have to 'come out' in the next. And this to happen over and over again, day after day, and no way for M to know what the reaction from the other person would be, whether it would be supportive and positive, merely curious, or emotionally, mentally or physically violent. I wonder how M felt about it, whether she would describe this as an example of insidious trauma.

The poems within this book, and *All the Men I Never Married* seek to capture my own experience of what it is to be traumatised by existence, to be, as Cathy Caruth puts it 'possessed by an image or event'[80], to live with repetition and circularity, because if sexism has anything at its centre, it is its propensity to repeat, repeat, repeat.

What happens when the reader is asked to look, and to look again, and to choose again to look at the things that most people look away from, or ignore? Even when sexism is happening to me, I have chosen to look away, to pretend nothing is happening and even this action is, as Brown writes, a reliance 'upon the defences of denial and minimization'[81]. Putting these experiences into the framework of a lyric poem ensures that I cannot rely on these defences anymore.

In *Theory of the Lyric,* Jonathan Culler defines the 'lyric convention of significance' as being a kind of unspoken agreement that the reader enters into or a shared understanding that 'the fact that something has been set down as a poem implies that it is important now, at the moment of lyric articulation, however trivial it might seem.'[82]

When experiences of sexism are placed into the framework of a lyric poem, the 'lyric convention of significance' comes into existence. It's hard to minimise an event when it is the centre of a poem. It's hard to minimise a moment in time as only a moment when it is placed into the lyric present.

Sara Ahmed wrote '[i]f a world can be what we learn not to notice, noticing becomes a form of political labor.'[83] I am writing poems that notice things. I am writing poems that recount the noticing of sexism, and in doing so, I become, as Ahmed writes, a 'retrospective witness of my own becoming.'[84] The naming of something as sexism often happens afterwards, when we look back. I feel a sense of responsibility towards what Adrienne Rich calls 'the project of describing our reality as candidly and fully as we can to each other.'[85]

In *Gendering Poetry*, Vicki Bertram writes that it is difficult for women poets to create a 'female lyric voice whose authority is accepted as transcending its femaleness to speak of general insights or truths.'[86] How can I create this voice, when the truth I am writing about is sexism, and sexism is often denied? Is it possible to transcend femaleness when writing about sexism? Is transcending femaleness something I want to aspire to anyway?

What I do know is that writing poetry about sexism and reading poems about sexism to an audience feels safer and easier than a conversation about sexism across a table or amongst friends. Somehow in a poem, there is more space to explore its impact on my daily lived experience, which perhaps I don't fully understand when I start writing, or even talking about it. In a poem, there is space to explore what I don't know I know, what I don't know I feel. The poem, by its very nature, invites such explorations.

Imagine this – I have just finished performing. I may have read poems about female desire, or an experience of sexism, or both. They will probably be poems about relationality, about how we relate to and fail each other. In that vulnerable moment after the reading, when the part of myself that chose to show itself, that chose to be looked at, is hiding deep inside once again, a man will come up to me and tell me how much he likes my hair, or my shoes, or my dress. These are compliments and I 'should' be flattered, but I am not, because they register as dismissals, as attempts to undermine me and my work. These dismissals fit with Ahmed's categorisation of sexism taking place under the language of 'civility, happiness and love'[87].

Bertram argues that women poets, in any performance of their work, have to 'confront the implications of being a woman on display.'[88] Often the implications and the cost of being a woman on display is that you are dismissed as a poet, and instead your body is addressed, and it is as if your work did not exist. I am put into my place as a person, a poet, reduced to a body.

Imagine this – I am giving a creative-critical reading of some of my PhD research. I've read the first paragraph and then a man puts his hand up, though he does not wait to be invited to speak. He tells me that sexism does not exist. It is exhausting to keep on insisting that something exists in a world which will not admit that it does exist. I repeat Ahmed's words, that merely by talking about 'sexism or racism here and now is to refuse displacement'[89]. I keep taking up space.

At the same event, another man tries to offer support when the first man continues to try and make his point. He tells the audience, and me, about a time when he had his bottom pinched when walking through a factory of female workers. He concludes that sexism does exist and that it works both ways. I am exhausted, even though I haven't really begun my lecture yet.

As discussed in 'Guilty for Being A Man' (page 67) analogies can be effective, but they can also wipe out or silence the experiences of already minoritized groups. In a discussion of how white people often use analogies to re-focus attention on themselves and appropriate pain in discussions about race, Grillo and Wildman write that 'The analogy makes the analogiser forget the difference and allows her to stay focused on her own situation without grappling the other person's reality.'[90] I wonder now if I am doing this very thing, by using this quote here, but I want – or need to talk about the man who raised his own experience of sexism. He was well-meaning, but his anecdote succeeded in what Grillo and Wildman call 'stealing the center'[91]. It has become apparent in the performing of poems which explore experiences of sexism that many men do not know how to respond except through defensiveness, compliments about my appearance, or false analogies that re-focus attention and time onto men, rather than onto women. I understand the impulse to analogise, because I also do this when I'm trying to understand racism, or transphobia, or homophobia, or ableism. It's a human reaction to try and make that connection between self and other, but perhaps it is not the most useful response.

Performing these poems, reading from creative-critical work is not a consciousness-raising session, and yet I have seen that these poems raise consciousness in both women and men. They have raised consciousness in myself. I return again to bell hooks and her call for 'new and radical speech'[92]. Can speech which contains information about sexism, whilst also uncovering sexism in the room be new and radical, or is it merely playing into those same patterns being re-enacted over and over again?

Or maybe I am asking the wrong questions. Do I trust poetry to be transformative or not? The act of performing poetry and the space of silence around a poem as it is read, or the publishing of a poem and the white space of silence on the printed page – is this enough, am I speaking in hooks' 'new and liberated voice'[93]? Maybe it's impossible to know what the right questions are when thinking about sexism. Every question risks missing another part of the puzzle. I can ask questions like 'Can poems about sexism raise consciousness about sexism?' and 'Can poems about sexism raise the consciousness we already have about sexism to the surface?' and 'What does our consciousness around sexism look like?' I could ask what transformation looks like, what does a new and liberated voice sound like, who am I talking to anyway, who am I looking at? Sexism is dynamic and embedded, fluid and static. It's all of these things, and so, asking questions – the wrong ones and the right ones – becomes an ethical aesthetical practice, to keep trying to articulate the shape of what is being missed.

If you have experienced sexism before, turn to 'Not Looking Away: A Poetics of Attention' on page 39.

If you have been a perpetrator of sexism, turn to 'Not Looking Away: A Poetics of Attention' on page 39.

If you would like to think about relationality instead, turn to 'Something in the Telling: A Poetics of Relationality' on page 84.

SOMETHING IN THE TELLING:
A POETICS OF RELATIONALITY

9.

Nothing has changed you still live with your gran
in a village where the lawns are edged with garden gnomes
it's a ten-minute walk to the canal which is so full
of water today I could reach over and stroke
its back so full another day's rain and it will be up
and over the sides how many years are you going
to show me your initials carved on the bridge
how many times will you tell me about the day
you were thrown into the water I no longer get
that clutch of fear at my throat when I think
of how you could have died before I met you
you are telling me again of how you toy
with the idea of living on a boat and I want to say
go on then do it or don't do it but don't
talk about it as if it's exciting talking about it
don't keep telling me you're tired again
you're sad again did you know I can't remember
your bedroom did you know this is the first time
I haven't wanted to touch your arm
for old times' sake remember one year
you helped me over the stile and left your hand
a second too long on my waist and I felt it again
the dizziness like vertigo but less dramatic
now you're telling me your ambition
is to get a twenty-two-year-old girlfriend
like your brother who has a problem with drink
and keeping a house clean but manages
you tell me to get a beautiful girl
or a *pretty little thing* as you call her
to sit on his knee and be all over him
I want to say do you ever wake up and worry

about becoming a cliché but I don't I can't
be bothered to keep being disappointed in you
and the way your beautiful animal face turned out

3.

we walked into the beginning of summer and crossed a motorway to get to the woods / you didn't care about fences or gates / we thought nobody had ever been there / the smell was earth and rotting leaves / the only sound the distant singing of the motorway / we ate humbugs from a paper bag / you killed the wasps that came to sketch their way around us / we wanted something to happen / we were too young to know something was happening

we walked through the middle of summer and ran away from a man who pulled out his floppy dick / and waved it apologetically in our direction / we walked to your house / you hated reading and writing / you hated school / but you'd built a pigeon loft from a map in your head / trained birds to fall from the sky to your hands / you taught me about rollers / you taught me about spinners / you taught me / about the naming of birds / you held an egg up to the light / what was inside looked like a baby / some days I wasn't allowed to see you

we walked towards the end of summer and lay down in a field / we let the sun make its way across the sky / did I imagine the man on horseback watching / as we rolled around in sweet-smelling grass / which trapped the heat / which hid us from the world / which hid us from everything but the sky / maybe my heart made him up / maybe my mind made him up / we were young / we stayed still as if staying still meant he wouldn't see / we covered our faces / you held my head to your shoulder / when we looked again there was no horseman / there was only you and I / do you remember the horseman?

30.

On the way from A wing to B wing
two prisoners start to circle each other

on the long corridor they call the high street,
where the leaves gather in corners.

They push their foreheads against each other,
their arms thrown back behind them.

The wind whistles past the canteen,
past closed doors, through the high grilled windows.

A guard shoves me through a gate, a hand
in the small of my back, locks it after us.

We watch men emerge from cells
and gather round the two still locked together.

It's like an old black-and-white silent movie
except even the black is a washed-out grey –

their jumpers and jogging bottoms,
the doors a darker shade, the walls

an almost-white, and just those leaves,
bright spots of colour, stirring a little

before they settle, brittle enough
to turn to dust if I could touch them

and not a sound from the men watching
or the two who are swinging at each other.

The alarm shrieks and prisoners drop to the ground
like fallen trees and we turn away.

Our men are waiting in the prison library
with poems on scraps of paper in their pockets.

Today Matt is leaving and Jack reads a poem,
tells him to never come back, forget they exist,

and Joe smiles like he's forgotten how,
and Luke says it rains in his mind, all the time,

and Arjun tells us about a country
where battles were fought with poems instead of swords.

They are listening, some with their eyes closed,
their heads cradled in their arms,

some with their eyes wide open.
When the bell calls them back to cells

they walk out of the room and are transformed,
back to fallen trees, or they become the wall

and never leave, or they change into a scrawl
of barbed wire and no one ever touches them again,

or they become the bars of a locked gate
and cast their shadows on each other,

they become the silence, they become the corridor
and men walk up and down inside.

40.

Also my ex and that first morning I woke up with him,
wasting it going to work but returning two hours later
to find him still there, the fresh new joy of it.

Also the smell of sex in the room, taking my clothes off again,
thinking there would be many days like it,
thinking there might not be a day like this again.

Also that he likes it when I talk about him this way.
Also how he only rang when he'd had a drink.
Also I understood even then about drink,

the way it makes passing truths seem things
you cannot do without. Also I was a passing truth
to him. He was a passing truth to me.

Also sadness at never using the body in that way again.
Also remembering the times I was angry with him.
Midnight and he's throwing stones at my window.

I'm playing Beethoven's 5th to drown out his voice.
Also not understanding how it had come to this,
from the bed and those mornings,

the press of bodies and skin, to this,
him out in the dark wearing my nightie
with my name on his chest.

Also realising it was a child's nightie (bear, flowers)
and the shame of not knowing that till then.
Also his numerous requests for nudes which I ignored.

Also Polly, asking whether I'd heard of the valley of shit,
me wanting to answer, I know someone who lives in it,
honey. But maybe I misheard.

Maybe she said something else entirely.
Also Polly, asking did I know that magpies
are actually scared of shiny things?

And me remembering the strange gleam of him
and wanting to keep him where I could see him,
under my eye, in my bed, between my legs.

The loneliness inside my chest and growing.
Also he called me miss graceful arms once in a text.
Also that my friends hated him.

Also that I swore he would never set foot in my flat again.
Also that stairwell. Stairs leading up to the roof
and that day slanting through my life like the brightest light.

Also that I left quickly, unhooked myself,
left him recovering himself, pulling himself together.
No, none of these, it was a gathering. Gathering himself in.

If you would like to read 'Doing Gender' turn to page 135.
If you would like to consider men, turn to 'Considering Men' on page 164.
If you would like to read 'Women's Images of Men – Desire, Vulnerability and
the Gaze' turn to page 119.

LYRIC VARIATIONS (1)

I'm sitting at a table with friends, friends I run with, who work in the shipyard or for the local council, the type of friends who run marathons and talk about running injuries and which races they are planning to attend, male friends who say things like 'Once my daughter is 16, that's it, I'm locking her up', friends who haven't thought about the way women's bodies are figured as owned, or that a father looking after a daughter's body and her sexuality, protecting/possessing it raises the question of what happens when they are not there to look after that body, that sexuality, friends who I would trust to walk me home late at night, friends who say 'Look! He's running like a woman!' and we all understand this as an insult, though they do not understand why I, or the other women present, might be hurt by these words.

Sometimes during such conversations I speak up. Sometimes I do not laugh when I am expected to. Sometimes I ask a question that is unexpected, that catches them by surprise. Sometimes I get angry or just disagree. Sometimes I pretend I did not hear what was said. Sometimes I remain silent. Strangely, it is easier to write a poem about sexism or stand up on stage and read a poem about sexism or publish a poem about sexism than it is to say something in the moment, at that table, to turn myself into what Sara Ahmed calls 'the feminist killjoy'[94] amongst a group of friends.

Why is it easier to talk about sexism and female desire in the space of a lyric poem? The answer might have something to do with what Jonathan Culler calls the co-operative principle. Drawing on Mary Louise Pratt's work on narrative in defining the co-operative principle as a shared agreement that each party is contributing something of significance to the conversation, Culler contends that in literature, the co-operative principle is 'hyper-protected'. Further, he asserts that the 'convention that whatever is written will prove to be important is particularly powerful, and crucial in the functioning of many modern lyrics especially.'[95]

This explains why poetry offers a powerful alternative to other forms when it comes to relaying sexism, which, as Sara Ahmed writes, often leads to the realisation that 'what you aim to bring to an end some do not recognise as existing'[96]. Even in poetry, of course, the co-operative principle cannot prevent an audience or reader from denying sexism, as can be seen from some of the responses recounted in this book. Still, poetry, with its heightened co-operative principle, does carve out a space for the words to be heard in the first place.

There are other ways in which the form of the lyric poem can support a writer seeking to transform experiences of sexism and trauma into language, which I will return to throughout this section, but first I want to unpack my use of the word 'lyric'.

While an outline of the history of the lyric poem falls beyond the scope of this book, it's useful to consider a brief overview of the context of the term and the ways it has been used to define a certain type of poetry, especially when considering how the contemporary lyric poem can engage with and extend these definitions and ideas about the lyric.

Historically, the lyric poem has been seen as being spoken by a unified 'lyric I' who is distinct from the poet. According to J.S. Mill, the lyric poem is always 'overheard' and is 'feeling confessing itself to feeling in moments of solitude'[97]. These ways of thinking about lyric poetry have persisted throughout history – as recently as 2006 the poet and critic Edward Hirsch described the lyric poem as a 'message in a bottle' and a 'solitude speaking to a solitude.'[98] These ideas are clearly influenced by Mill, but also more recently by Paul Celan, who Hirsch discusses at length in his 1999 *How To Read A Poem (And Fall In Love with Poetry)*.

Mill argues that the moment the poet addresses another, when 'the act of utterance is not itself the end, but a means to an end' then 'it ceases to be poetry, and becomes eloquence'[99]. As I understand it, Mill is arguing here for the elevation of sound over the delivery of information. In contrast to this, for Hirsch, the reader (or the addressee) is of paramount importance. He writes that reading a poem is a 'particular kind of exchange between two people not physically present to each other.'[100] This idea of exchange, of something being given and received by *both* parties seems to be crucial to Hirsch's ideas of what lyric poetry can be or do.

The New Critic school of criticism was built on the premise of the text as 'closed', meaning that anything needed to understand or interpret a work can be found within the text, and that biography or influences have little relevance to its literary merit. The prevailing conception of the 'speaker' of the poem as distinct from the poet was, according to Gillian White, 'consolidated and codified at mid-century by the New Critics'[101]. This idea of a unified lyric speaker, who is able to elevate personal experience to the universal, has led to criticism directed at the lyric in general in terms of the space it affords marginalised poets. In a 2017 edition of *Poetry London,* poets Sandeep Parmar and Bhanu Kapil argue that the lyric is a hostile space for writers who do not fit into the 'shared assumptions about experience, language and tradition.'[102]

Another widespread criticism levelled at lyric poetry is that it is 'merely' personal, rather than universal, a criticism also often directed at marginalised writers and women writers in particular. I have personally faced this criticism when publishing my work and have explored this more thoroughly in the essay 'The Annihilation of Men' (page 154).

These assumptions are based on the premise that lyric poetry *should* elevate from the personal to the universal. A more interesting proposition might be if we engaged with lyric poetry in a different way. Luce Irigaray talks about the space between people – or the 'between-us'[103] as being an important part of relationality. Could the 'between-us' become part of our mode of engagement with poetry? This would involve not drawing an analogy from the poem to our own lives or experience but instead being willing to sit or examine the 'between-us', which might involve sitting with and in discomfort.

If we did not expect to identify with every poem, but instead explored and examined what goes on when a poem isolates or annoys or connects with us, our reading practices would be enriched. In Adrienne Rich's poem 'Trying to Talk With A Man' she starts 'Out here we are testing bombs.'[104] Could we think of a lyric poem as a bomb being tested, as a way of testing ourselves and each other, rather than recognising (or not) our similarities?

This desire to be similar, or to make a connection is very human but it reduces a poem's worth to its relatability. Helen Vendler writes that she hopes readers of lyric poetry will say '[h]eavens, I recognise the place, I know it!', (quoting a central line from Elizabeth Bishop's 'Poem'). Vendler continues 'It is the effect every poet hopes.'[105]

Alternatively, Charles Bernstein states in the 'Artifice of Absorption' that he hopes that readers might say of some poems, 'Hell, I don't recognise the place or the time, or the 'I' in this sentence. I don't know it.'[106] Bernstein was criticising the mainstream lyric tradition as he saw it, but his understanding of the definition and function of lyric poetry seems restrictive in a different way. In fact, any understanding of the lyric that has been outlined here so far – that it is a 'solitude speaking to solitude', that it can only ever be something 'overheard', or , that it should be recognisable or familiar in some way, or that lyric poetry is spoken by a single, unified speaker who does not need to address or take notice of an audience seems simplistic, reductive and doomed to failure. Any lyric poem must after all, reach across the boundary of the body, and be received by another's body, so the concept of the lyric poem as a 'message in a bottle', divorced from time, meaning and place seems a strange one to say the least.

White argues that the qualities outlined above, generally thought of as belonging to lyric poetry, are not actually features of the form, but 'lyric-reading assumptions' and that we are all engaged in a 'lyric-reading culture together'[107]. She

contests that both writers and readers of lyric poetry experi-
ence 'lyric shame' which centres around our preconceived idea
of a coherent, expressive and above all truthful lyric *I*.

White uses the example of Anne Sexton to dismantle
assumptions about lyric poetry and so-called 'confessional'
poetry. Although Sexton's poetry is often described as highly
personal and criticised on these grounds, White calls attention
to the way that Sexton knowingly experiments with the space
between the speaker in the poem and the audience and be-
tween the speaker in the poem and the poet.

According to White, it is this experiment that makes Sex-
ton's work 'shameful'. The audience can no longer be 'invisible
listeners' and instead are turned into intimated readers 'caught'
in the act as 'unseemly voyeurs'.[108] White contests that Sexton's
poems 'draw on, foreground, and complicate the very fiction
of 'voicing' and 'overhearing' that are important to the con-
ventional constructions of lyric.[109] These conventional
constructions were widespread in the time Sexton was writing,
making her approach truly radical.

It could be argued that all lyric poetry 'outs' both its author
and its audience. Poets end up appearing from behind the
curtain of language whether they want to or not, and in our
own act of perception and our reading, we end up outing
ourselves, too.

As White points out throughout *Lyric Shame*, the binary be-
tween the lyric tradition and the avant-garde and
LANGUAGE poetries is a misleading one. These labels are
often used to fall back on when definitions of genre are at-
tempted, which only serve to narrow and constrict the
possibilities of what the lyric can do.

The lyric poems I am interested in writing trouble and
challenge these 'lyric-reading assumptions'. Many of the
poems in my second collection *All the Men I Never Married*
experiment with modes of address by addressing the audience
or reader directly. In 'Yes, I Am Judging You' (page 28) I talk
about what happened when I read aloud a poem that directly

addressed the audience halfway through, and the discomfort of being heckled. At the time of writing the early drafts of that poem, I hadn't been thinking in particular about lyric address. I remember feeling alarmed when I wrote the question 'Are you surprised, are you judging me yet?' I was suddenly brought up short, aware of myself and my own judgement. Yes, I answer myself. Yes, I am surprised.

The direct address, the direct question at the heart of this poem is one thing when it is received by a reader – or as Hirsch puts it, one solitude speaking to another solitude. In the act of performance, when I ask this question of an audience, of a group – the poem finds its completion by another route. I always feel some kind of exchange in the air – a puzzling out of what it means to judge, or be judged.

Charles Bernstein writes that in lyric poetry, the 'fourth wall' convention is upheld, in that '[n]othing in the text should cause self-consciousness about the reading process: it should be as if the writer & the reader are not present.'[110] But whenever I read any pronouncements about what lyric poetry 'should' do, I want to say – yes, of course it can. I want to say – but it doesn't have to.

This 'lyric-reading assumption' that the fourth wall must be maintained means that when an audience or reader feels themselves addressed, then the bedrock of ideas around lyric poetry starts to shift under their feet. The lyric is no longer addressed to an unseen listener. It can no longer be thought of as an accidental overhearing. Instead, White argues that audience and readers suddenly experience a 'sudden, problematic awareness of their own mediating presence as readers'[111]. The first time this happened to me was reading Rainer Maria Rilke's 'Archaic Torso of Apollo'[112].

In the final line of the poem, Rilke writes 'You must change your life', and on reading this, I felt something change inside me. Is he talking directly to the person reading the poem, or to a wider audience, or to himself? The shift in the last line, the way the 'you' hovers with no fixed recipient, the way that line is so full of possibility made me feel as if *I* was full of possibility, as if my life was, as if it was something I had the power to change. I wonder now if the energy of the turn in this poem to direct address was at the back of my mind when I wrote the poem that is threaded through the essay 'Yes, I Am Judging You' (page 28).

And what did I do with this life that I suddenly realised I had the power to change? I applied for funding to do a PhD and left my old life as a music teacher behind me, and wrote *All the Men I Never Married,* and this book. Of course it is simplistic to say it all came from reading Rilke's poem, but perhaps it jumpstarted me into action, or caused me to act sooner rather than later.

Gillian White's assertion that a poem can create a 'sudden, problematic awareness' for readers and audiences fascinated me enough to want to experiment with the idea in 'All the Men I Never Married No. 7' (page 41). I wanted to see what it felt like to break that fourth wall from the first line, to directly address the audience or reader, asking them to 'Imagine you're me', knowing the hopeful, hopelessness of that invitation.

This ability of the lyric to turn to and address the audience or reader directly is an important tool when writing about sexism and female desire, because of its potential to enlist the reader into different positions of spectator, witness, survivor or even perpetrator. It's an important tool, and yet it's only one of many techniques that make lyric poetry a potentially more useful space than prose to examine sexism.

Jonathan Culler argues that the most important features of lyric poetry is its use of 'triangulated address', where the audience or readers are addressed through someone else, whether this is a 'lover, a god, natural forces or personified abstractions'[113]. The apostrophic figure is particularly important in *All the Men I Never Married,* in that many of the poems are addressed to a 'you' and inhabit the traditional 'overheard' character of the lyric poem. Put another way, the 'gaze' of the poem is directed toward an unseen 'you', but often swings away from this 'you' to look back at the audience, breaking Bernstein's 'fourth wall.'

Culler also argues that the hypberbolic quality of the lyric should not be underestimated. It means that lyric can 'risk investing mundane occurrence with meaning'[114]. In terms of writing about an everyday occurrence of sexism, it's clear that the act of putting white space around an experience of sexism elevates the everyday and makes it worthy of reflection and consideration, meaning that even small instances of sexism become impossible to dismiss as 'nothing' or not meaningful.

Writing about nothing is not what it seems. The co-operative principle, heightened in a lyric poem, invites the reader to enter into an agreement that its content is of high value, and worth listening to. The lyric poem can relay an incident or anecdote without explaining its importance, relying on what Culler calls the 'lyric convention of significance: the fact that something has been set down as a poem implies that it is important now, at the moment of lyric articulation, however trivial it might seem.'[115]

It is then, the white space and line breaks of a lyric poem that call into existence the lyric convention of significance. Experiences and moments can be told in prose, but there is always a moving on to the next thing happening. In a lyric poem, the reader is asked to pause and consider. The white space makes the content harder to minimise or discount, and yet the white space signifies silence, the place where language has failed in some way, the place where time makes its presence felt. When Sara Ahmed writes that '[t]he past is magnified when it is no longer shrunk. We make things bigger just by refusing to make them smaller'[116] it can be seen that the inherent structure of the lyric poem supports this magnification.

Not only is the content of a lyric poem assumed to be significant because of its form, Susan S. Lanser argues that [l]yric poetry, with its 'conventional singularity, its commonplace anonymity, its almost axiomatic reliability, its likelihood of evoking aspects of its authors identity, and its relatively low narrativity, is primed for authorial attachment.'[117] She argues that the emotional truth of the poem is what readers attach to the author, rather than the specific events or situations used to illustrate this emotional truth. This feature of lyric poetry is another example of why it is a useful form for examining experiences of sexism, violence and trauma.

If you would like to read 'Lyric Variations (2) turn to page 106.

If you are not sure whether sexism exists, turn to 'Sexism is a Slippery and Fluid Term' on page 76.

If you are interested in what we choose to look at in poetry, turn to 'Intimate Witness: A Poetics of Watching' on page 140.

INSIDIOUS TRAUMA:
A BIOGRAPHY OF VIOLENCE

11.

Once I knew a man who thought he knew everything. I often returned from work to find him asleep in my bed. It was like the sun had slipped itself between the sheets, or a lion, or something else born golden and sure of itself. Even though I knew all the stories about finding people in your bed, how it always ended badly – the three bears, the little girl with the red cape – what could I do but climb in beside him? He must have spent hours shaving his chest and back so that women like me could slide along him, as if we were bodies of water and he the dry and thirsty earth. The man who thought he knew everything never learnt that he didn't, and I realised too late. This was why he was the way he was, as if he'd been touched and turned to gold by a foolish, laughing king.

12.

After the reading a man waits around to tell me the poem I read about a beautiful man who thought he knew everything was objectifying men – how would it feel if the gender of the protagonist was reversed he says triumphantly – I reply that it would feel like most other love poems in the course of human history – he says aha! so this is really a very ordinary subject – I say yes if you discount subversion and poetic tradition and female desire – more accurately I only get to subversion and poetic tradition and female de... before he interrupts me to tell me how disappointed he is as I'm a better writer than this wasting my talent making cheap shots about men – the man in my poem does spend the whole poem naked so maybe he is a little bit objectified – but I like him that way – I start to write a poem about the opinionated man who is busy shaking his head at my misunderstanding of beautiful men and their complex desires which I've only skimmed over in my original poem by not giving my man a voice of his own – not allowing him to tell his own story – I'm about to make a general and sweeping statement about men when he interrupts again – isn't the man in your poem a bit one-dimensional he opines – can't you make him more interesting – just trying to be helpful he says holding his hands up like two little flags – like two dish-cloths – like two dead moles hung on a fence – I reply no I can't – that is the best thing about him – or maybe I'm just wishing I said that – maybe I just smiled – nodded my head

20.

It's just me and him, alone in the staffroom
and he's talking about a colleague he hates.

*I bet she has a big pubic mound. I bet
it's covered in spider's legs.*

He's already on about the next thing wrong
with his life, his job, with this woman.

I'm thinking about the women I know,
how good they are at getting rid of things,

experts in the endurance of pain.
Look at me now for example, sitting here

not moving a muscle as I remember
taking a razor to my upper lip

because the boys at school called me names.
My mum saying *what have you done?*

*You're too young for all this. Once you start
you can't stop, there's no going back.*

After that there was bleach, the flame of it
on my skin, testing myself –

how long could I stand it, how much
could I make disappear.

Then electrolysis, a needle into each follicle
and one dark hair at a time wished away.

Back in the staffroom he's saying
the next time someone annoys me

I should *flash them my tits,*
miming the action while making a cuppa.

Milk, no sugar, I say with a smile
I hate myself for. I remember all the times

I heard that as a teenager. *Get your tits out
for the lads.* It sounds obscene now

but back then it was nothing, just one
of the things that boys said.

In my first class of the morning
a boy asks why I have hair on my lip.

My stomach still drops like it used to
but I answer calmly this time.

All women do. Your mum probably does.
He looks outraged, maybe doesn't believe me

and how can I blame him?
This is not what they told him

about bodies and women
and I long for the staffroom

and the easy misogyny
and the laughing along with it all.

2.

Many years ago, I lived in a house in the woods.
The woodcutter visited on nights when the moon
hid itself between the clouds.

Sometimes I go back to watch it happen again,
slip inside the body of the woodcutter,
to feel what it felt like to be him.

His arms and legs are heavier than mine.
The cigarettes on his heart, his lungs, his chest.
His finger to his lips, biting the nail to the quick.

I start to lose the border of where
his pain and mine begin and end.
I am in the body of the woodcutter.

But I am not the body of the woodcutter.
His body is a shallow dish and I'm a slick of water.
If I move too much, I'll spill out and over.

What I've really come back for is me,
ten years younger. Through his eyes,
she looks small and pale, a wisp of smoke

he could walk right through. Her face
turned in. Her mouth shut tight.
She smells of flight and all the things

this body hates. But when he presses her
to the ground, she vanishes inside herself
and nobody can reach her.

His tongue spits words I'd never say, and yet
here I am, inside his body saying them.
I leave the body of the woodcutter.

I leave it all behind – her, the house, the trees.
I return to myself, begin again.

Many years ago, I lived in a house in the woods.

If you would like to read 'All the Men I Never Married No.46' turn to page 153.
If you have lyric-reading assumptions, turn to 'Lyric Variations (1)' on page 91.

LYRIC VARIATIONS (2)

'All the Men I Never Married No. 2' (page 104) plays with and exploits many of the tropes and tools of the lyric poem. One of these tropes is the tendency of poems to call into being or be in conversation with other poems about the same subject. A poem about a fox may conjure up in the mind of the reader 'The Thought Fox' by Ted Hughes or a poem about a bird singing may recall John Keats 'Ode to a Nightingale'.

'All the Men I Never Married No. 2' inhabits the language and the world of fairy tales, making use of familiar tropes such as a woodcutter and a house in the woods. The woodcutter is a perpetrator in this poem, and this twist on the usual story puts the poem into conversation with other more subversive versions and retellings such as Carol Ann Duffy's poem, 'Little Red-Cap'. Duffy's poem is a feminist retelling of the story of Little Red Riding Hood and has always been a favourite poem of mine.

Little Red-Cap (Duffy's Red Riding Hood) follows the wolf willingly into the woods, entering into a relationship char-acterised by sexual desire and built on a love of language. In Duffy's version, the wolf's lair is depicted as having 'a whole wall … crimson, gold, aglow with books.'[118] The woodcutter, usually cast as saviour and rescuer in the traditional telling of the fairy tale does not feature at all in Duffy's poem – instead it is Little Red-Cap who takes the woodcutter's axe and kills the wolf, finding her literal and literary ancestor inside his belly in the form of her grandmother's bones. Here we see that Little Red-Cap does not need the patriarchal protection of the woodcutter and instead rescues herself.

Duffy's poem starts 'At childhood's end', which was where I was when I read this poem for the first time. I was living away from home, studying trumpet at music college. The figure of the older, powerful, alluring male was one that many young female musicians in my generation had to negotiate and find our way around or through, so this poem contained multiple resonances for me, resonances that I am still listening for today, over twenty years later.

It took me nearly twenty years to write 'All the Men I Never Married No. 2', and although the speaker in this poem is not Little Red Riding Hood, perhaps her spirit runs through this poem by its absence, or is conjured up because of the associations with the character and woodcutters, with houses, with forests. When I trace the roots of this poem back, I am sure that deeply embedded within it is this Duffy poem.

The figure of the woodcutter is absent in Duffy's poem, or represented only by the axe. In contrast, the woodcutter in my poem is a controlling and violent perpetrator. Aside from the common ground of the landscape of fairy tales, both poems ask questions about the idea of rescue – who can be rescued, who can be the rescuer, and what is the meaning of rescue.

In their 2004 article 'Bad but bold: ambivalent attitudes towards men predict gender inequality in 16 nations' Glick et al. identified two types of sexism – benevolent sexism and hostile sexism. Hostile sexism is perhaps self-explanatory, covering hostility 'towards women who challenge male power'. Benevolent sexism is more complex and encompasses 'attitudes that are subjectively benevolent but patronising, casting women as wonderful but fragile creatures who ought to be protected and provided for by men.'[119] There have been numerous studies which have found a correlation between high levels of benevolent and hostile sexism, proving that these two types of sexism are interconnected and support each other.

According to the national charity Refuge, 1 in 3 women in the UK will experience domestic violence during their lifetimes. It often starts with benevolent sexism – a jealous partner will be seen as being protective rather than possessive. Fairy tales full of fathers/woodcutters 'protecting' daughters or young women configured as weaker feed into tolerance, and celebration of benevolent sexism as a positive thing. This connection between these two types of sexism is something I wanted to examine in this poem. In the same way that Duffy transforms the figure of the wolf and Little Red-Cap into much more complex figures than their fairy tale counterparts, I wanted to reach for a new understanding of the woodcutter.

Cathy Caruth argues that the impact of trauma is in its 'refusal to be simply located, in its insistent appearance outside the boundaries of any single place or time.'[120] In this poem, I wanted to experiment with portraying the time-shifting nature of trauma with a speaker who returns again and again to the place and site of trauma through memory, language and the senses.

Despite this poem drawing on the language of fairy tale, utilizing archetypes such as the woodcutter and deploying surrealist descriptions of going back in time and entering the body of another, I think of this poem as highly auto-biographical. It is firmly anchored to the emotional truth of what it was like for me to experience trauma and be unable to move past it, to live with what Caruth calls a 'breach in the mind's experience of time'[121].

In his 2002 book *Poetry As Survival,* the poet Gregory Orr imagines the lyric poem as a 'threshold between disorder and order', linking the threshold with a doorsill or doorway and going as far as to compare the rectangular shape of the page to 'a doorframe in which we seek shelter.' He writes that '[i]t is on a threshold, at the edge, where we are most able to alter our understanding of the world and of our own lives in it.'[122] This poem was a 'threshold' poem for me, in that the act of writing it helped me to shape an experience and alter my understanding of the world and my own life. Writing the poem helped me think through the ways that my experience of benevolent sexism had taught me to accept hostile sexism when it arrived, to be gradually swallowed up by it.

Having said I think of this poem as autobiographical, I should also add that I did not want to tell the story, or the content of the traumatic event that lies behind this poem. What I was interested in, and remain interested in is the process of trauma, and the processing of it. I wanted to articulate in language what Caruth's 'breach in the mind's experience of time' feels like.

Jonathan Culler writes that lyric poems are rarely in the past tense, because 'the past tense is a narrative tense'[123]. What is more common is for the lyric poem to begin in the past and move to the present, or as Culler puts it, the past is 'explicitly pulled into the lyric present'[124]. 'All the Men I Never Married No. 2' follows this convention, moving from the past to the present, before the lyric present is pulled backwards into the past. As Culler specifies, the lyric poem is 'not timeless but a moment of time that is repeated every time the poem is read.'[125] What does it mean for a poet, what does it mean for a reader or an audience to be asked to repeat a moment of time, a journey, to be asked to look, and look again, and not look away, when what they are looking at is trauma?

In the same way that Rosalind Gill, in her 2011 essay 'Sexism Reloaded, or, It's Time To Get Angry Again' calls for a new definition of sexism as an 'agile, dynamic, changing and diverse set of malleable representations and practices of power'[126], perhaps a new conceptualisation of what lyric poetry is and can be is needed, perhaps as a series of variations rather than a form with a linear history.

There is room and scope for the lyric poem to be a potent, radical and change-making space in which to discuss experiences of sexism. One possibility is to re-vision the lyric and draw on its history as rooted in ancient Greece, as discourse that 'aims to praise or persuade' or as Culler puts it, as 'epideictic discourse'[127].

The poet Carolyn Forché used the term 'poetry of witness' to describe poetry that combines the personal, political and the social. In the introduction to the anthology *Against Forgetting: Twentieth-Century Poetry of Witness* she writes '[t]he distinction between the personal and the political gives the political realm too much and too little scope; at the same time, it renders the personal too important and not important enough...We need a third term, one that can describe the space between the state and the supposedly safe havens of the personal. Let us call this space "the social".'[128]

It may seem inappropriate to include poetry written about sexism under the heading of 'poetry of witness', but maybe this is that tendency to minimise again. In her introduction, Forché says that she 'decided to limit the poets in the anthology to those for whom the social had been invaded by the political in ways that were sanctioned neither by law nor by the fictions of the social contract'[129]. Experiences of sexism and gender-based violence and misogyny are examples of how the personal is invaded by both the political and the social, so maybe 'poetry of witness' is an apt description for poems that explore experiences of sexism.

Poet and academic Mary Jean Chan refers to *Citizen* by Claudia Rankine as a text that bears 'intimate witness to racial injustice'[130]. Can lyric poetry be the threshold, the doorway to bear intimate witness to gender-based violence, misogyny and what Maria Root defines as the 'insidious trauma'[131] which follows? In her essay 'Outside the Range' Laura Brown argues that all women who live in a culture with a high incidence of rape and sexual assault know and understand that they could be attacked at any time. Consequently we live in a state of 'rape trauma' – some of the ways this manifests include hypervigilance and avoidance of high risk situations. Brown argues that these manifestations of trauma are often managed by coping strategies which include minimization and denial.[132]

One technique that Claudia Rankine uses throughout *Citizen* to examine micro-aggressions and racist behaviours and structures is the use of micro-observation – the act of paying attention to small, everyday interactions and details, closely linked with techniques of literary realism. Rankine examines these small-scale social scenes, and shows how they are part of a larger structural and societal pattern of racism. This makes it impossible to deny or minimise the impact of micro-aggressions.

The academic Heather Love argues that micro-observation challenges 'assumptions about the political significance of the micro scale.[133]' Criticisms of this kind of granular observation point out that it can in some instances lead to an endorsement of the status quo in its reflection or replication of reality. The sociologist Erving Goffman, in a discussion of his research methodology of micro-observation, writes 'I can only suggest that he who would combat false consciousness and awaken people to their true interests has much to do, because sleep is very deep. And I do not intend here to provide a lullaby but merely to sneak in and watch the way people snore.'[134]

Thankfully, the act of writing a poem is not like watching people snore. Writing in itself makes this kind of deep sleep of false consciousness impossible for me. Writing is like ringing a bell to wake me up from deep sleep, or to return to Gregory Orr's metaphor once again, allows me to stand and look out at the world differently, through a new door, on the 'threshold between disorder and order'[135].

For example, in 'All the Men I Never Married No. 4' (page 43), I started off writing about a strange experience at a party. I didn't realise what the poem was really about until I finished, or more accurately, until I performed the poem at an event. Faced with the reaction of the audience, I could no longer use minimization or denial to avoid calling what happened an assault.

I started writing 'All the Men I Never Married No.23' (page 142) and genuinely believed it was going to be a 'funny' poem. Laughter of course, is another common coping mechanism and a way to minimize what happened. It was reading the poem aloud to an audience that allowed me to understand the gravity of what I was writing about. It sounds obvious now to say it, but any type of stalking is no laughing matter.

It may seem like a contradiction in terms to be in both a deep sleep of false consciousness *and* hypervigilance because of what Laura Brown calls 'rape trauma'. I believe both states are possible, particularly if the reasons you are in a state of hypervigilance are denied, avoided or justified. I would also argue that the act of using micro-observation and placing these social scenes into the framework of a lyric poem gives them significance and importance, with the form of the lyric itself making it impossible to merely endorse the status quo. The 'everyday' becomes, as Love defines it, a 'significant site for the recognition and negotiation of race, gender, class and sexual inequality.'[136]

The hyperbolic quality of the lyric means that an image, such as William Carlos Williams' red wheelbarrow[137], can inspire an epiphany in the reader. Using lyric poetry to write about experiences of sexism does not replicate the world as it is – it holds up a moment in time and asks the reader to look at the world as it was, and as it is in the lyric present. Once this moment is made significant, something is changed, and if something is changed, nothing can be the same again, and both reader and writer must make a decision as to what they do with this new-found knowledge.

Robert M. Emerson, a scholar of ethnography identifies three types of responses to 'ordinary troubles.' These are 'managerial responses', where the complainant responds in 'ways that avoid or minimize confrontation'; 'dyadic complaints', where the complainant 'directly complains to and confronts the other...usually in cautious and moderated fashion', and 'distancing and extreme responses', which are 'systematic avoidance and/or strongly antagonistic punitive actions taken toward the other.'[138]

I recognise my own responses to sexism as mainly managerial responses in my everyday life. These could be choosing to walk a different way, laughing at something I do not think is funny, minimising something so that it does not upset me, or pretending not to notice or hear something. The marked characteristic of managerial responses is that the person who has caused them often does not notice the impact of their behaviour.

Does it help me to theorise my responses to sexism, to have a name for it? Yes, and no. Whether I will respond differently now in everyday life is unpredictable, but writing lyric poetry about experiences of sexism is a response that does not seem to fall into any of Emerson's categories. It's not a direct complaint and confrontation of the other. It can't be, unless the individual who inspired the poem is in the audience or reading the book and recognised the incident as something they were part of. It's not a punitive response in that nothing bad is going to happen to the other. However, the lyric poem asks the reader to generalise from the individual to the social, so although it is not a direct confrontation with the other as an individual, perhaps it can confront what Audre Lorde termed the 'oppressor which is planted deep within each of us'.

Lyric poetry as documentation, as a biography of violence, as feminist work. Lyric poetry as testimony, as intimate witnessing. Lyric poetry as social engagement, as epideictic discourse, as persuasion, as praise, as a path from past-to-present, from present-to-past. Lyric poetry as relational, as between-us, as a way of looking. Lyric poetry as micro-observation, as experiential, as personal, as political, as social, as rooted in history, as a repeating moment in time, as a way of generating empathy. Lyric poetry as a beautiful failure, as a container of silence, as a holder of the long, slow sounds, the echoes. Lyric poetry as holder of symbol, of image. Lyric poetry as space where these things slide away or shatter or never existed at all. Lyric poetry as place of transformation for the reader, for the writer. Lyric as the place where nothing transforms at all.

If you would like to read 'Something in the Telling: A Poetics of Relationality' turn to page 84.

If you would like to read 'To Give an Account of the Self' turn to page 169.

If you would like to read 'Yes, I Am Judging You' turn to page 28.

POEMS OF DESIRE: A MODE OF ATTENTION

14.

I imagine you at home on the other side of the world
in a town I don't know the name of, driving your wife mad,

leaving your laptop in the fridge as you go to get a beer.
It's hot. You're wearing shorts and a dark t-shirt.

Your white feet look like two fish washed up on a beach
and gasping their last breath. I know this although

I've not seen your feet in this life. The last time we met
you were fully clothed, black jacket, jeans, but now

without them, I can see you stand with a stoop,
your shoulders hunched, your body apologetic.

You are singing something I can't make out, your high
thin voice threads through the window and across

time zones and oceans to me here. When I think
of your voice, my soul drifts downwards inside my body

like a leaf falling side to side through the air.
Remember that night we were leaning into each other

like two doors loosening from their hinges?
Remember the darkness and how we almost

held hands? It wasn't even that I wanted to.
But I didn't not want to. It was complicated.

15.

I knew he was dangerous, that he had a girlfriend
he'd been with for years before he left her behind,
easy as slipping off a coat, knew that was a bad sign
but didn't know enough to keep my distance,
to not pick up the phone when his name appeared.
Oh I knew nothing back then, I thought sex was a promise
that would keep being fulfilled, I thought love was a knife
pressed to the throat, I thought there was a blade
in each of our hands. I am telling this now so he appears,
as real as that first night when we didn't sleep.
The slight red stubble of his beard, the freckles
covering his arms – his gaze, his attention all mine –
oh back then I never wanted it to end, the touching,
the looking, I didn't know that a person is already fractured
by the time that we meet them. It was just like Rilke said,
his gaze was a lamp turned low, although in those days
I knew nothing about what it was to be seen, what it means
to change or be changed, to appear, to burst like a star.

18.

This is not love. We are not speaking of love.
We are singing of Hardy: *Woman much missed,*
how you call to me, call to me – we are speaking
only of this. Outside I shout the whole thing

into the wind. There is darkness between us,
there is the ocean. My lips are moving
but nothing is heard. This is not love but it is
something like it. Here we are with the loyalty

of clouds. We are drifting, two boats on the water.
You have the wild in you, little wolf.
This is what happens when the body is a boat
and the heart is high and bright as a lantern.

35.

You are telling me about the city, about the city starving,
about the siege and forgive me for only half-listening,

until you mention the woman with the cigarette
held between her fingers then quick between her lips,

how she stubbed each one out again and again,
her hair covering her shoulders. Forgive me for thinking

of her face when you're talking about the city,
about the city starving, forgive me for concentrating

on her skin, the woman with the nervous smile,
the woman with the sibilant name. All I can imagine

is her hair covering her shoulders, while outside
your city dwindled to nothing, forgive me for not asking

how you survived in there. It's true that at first
I was distracted by your eyes until you mentioned

the woman then she bloomed in my mind,
her bare shoulders, her long hair and now I know

something is ending when you say make love
and I say sex, but either way I realise I don't want to,

or more accurately I don't want to stop wanting it,
I'd rather stay here, poised on this edge with you,

neither one thing or the other, a beautiful balancing trick,
half-knowing nothing, half-knowing your body,

and please carry on looking at me in that way,
I feel unclothed when you do, just for you,

though not nude, but naked with you in this space.
But don't assume I'm the woman in that place.

If I'm anything, I'm the cigarette, burning.
And you are the city. And you are starving.

If you do not want to look away, turn to 'Not Looking Away: A Poetics of Attention' on page 39.
If you are interested in what can happen to the female poet when performing, turn to 'The Body is the Blindspot of Speech' on page 145.

WOMEN'S IMAGES OF MEN – DESIRE, VULNERABILITY AND THE GAZE

In 1980 an exhibition called *Women's Images of Men* appeared at the Institute of Contemporary Art in London. It was organised by a collective of women artists which included Jacqueline Morreau, Catherine Elwes, Pat Whiteread and Joyce Agee. In the subsequent book *Women's Images of Men*, published by Pandora Press in 1985, editors Sarah Kent and Jacqueline Morreau elaborate on some of the aims of the exhibition in their essay 'Lighting a Candle'. These aims included finding out 'what women's attitudes towards men were' and highlighting the 'substantial group of women artists…using figuration and narrative to explore their ideas.'[139] In this essay, they elaborate further, stating that at the time of the exhibition, the use of figurative techniques was rejected by both the feminist avant-garde and the male mainstream.

This exhibition, on what Kent and Morreau described as the 'hidden subject of men'[140] was a huge success and attracted audiences of over a thousand people per day, breaking all previous attendance records at the ICA. However, it was the reaction of the critics that was most noteworthy. In her essay 'Looking Back' in *Women's Images of Men*, Sarah Kent recounts some of these reactions. Of the ninety-eight works exhibited, twenty were male nudes, and only two of those featured representations of a penis or genital area. Despite this, the exhibition was described as a 'veritable forest of penises' by Marina Vaizey in the *Sunday Times*. It's interesting, but perhaps not surprising that this inaccurate depiction of the overall subject matter of the exhibition came from a female critic. Internalized misogyny is a well-known and acknowledged effect of living in a patriarchal and misogynist society. Male critics were not far behind either in communicating their disdain – Terence Mullaly, writing in the *Daily Telegraph*, described the female artists as 'overwrought ladies' who thought of 'nothing but the male's sex organs', whilst Philip

Midgeley, writing for the *Times Educational Supplement*, saw nothing but a 'shrill scream of pain and frustration'[141].

Looking back at the exhibition through the lens of the book of the same name, and with the vantage point of forty years, it's striking how so many of the concerns and themes explored are still relevant and being fought/thought over today. Sometimes it feels as if nothing has changed from that moment in the 1980s, which so alarmed the (mostly) male critics and the art establishment.

For example, in her essay 'Looking Back' Sarah Kent points out that 'A woman who refuses to avert her eyes in the social or academic worlds and insists on speaking out risks ridicule or violence even today.'[142] When I read these words, I felt a painful stab of recognition. In the course of my own 'looking', my own 'speaking out', I have experienced ridicule, dismissal, denial, minimization and insults, although I am thankful that none of this has extended to actual physical violence. It's both depressing and fascinating to me that Kent's words are as true today in 2023 as when she wrote them in 1990.

When a woman speaks out about sexism, the cry of 'Not All Men' will often (soon) be heard. *Some* men see a woman looking at a man, hear her talking about him, and feel defensive, because to them, every man is an Everyman. In *The Work of Fire*, Maurice Blanchot writes that 'the question which kept interrogating the writer while he was writing – though he may not have been aware of it – is now present on the page; and now the same question lies silent within the work...'[143]. The question I thought I was asking was how to use lyric poetry to write about sexism and female desire, but there is another question haunting this book, these essays, these poems, this language, which is: what happens when men are looked at, when they are placed as the object of the gaze? What happens to you, and what happens to me?

In her book *The Poethical Wager*, J. Retallack defines 'poethics' as an 'attempt to note and value traditions in art exemplified by a linking of aesthetic registers to the fluid and rapidly changing experiences of everyday life.'[144] Retallack's concept of 'poethics' is helpful in terms of my own creative practice in that it calls for art that is constantly in conversation with our lives. When Retallack writes that '[l]iterature (in contrast to journal writing) is an entry into public conversation'[145], I agree with her, and when I read '[w]ho knows what might lead some *us* or another to become better at transfiguration than re-enactment'[146], I feel shame, and I feel hope at the same time, because I know that although the poems included here and in *All the Men I Never Married* invite re-enactment, they also offer space for transformation, for both myself and readers and audiences. I know that I have been transformed in the writing of them. I also know I have re-enacted, re-lived past trauma, past violations in both the writing and performing of these poems. I have uncovered sexism in the room and I could not make it leave. Blanchot tells us that with the act of writing you can be certain that 'what bursts into the light is none other than what was sleeping in the night'[147] and this truth plays out every time I perform these poems.

Kent argues that 'the right to look is equated with sexual dominance', pointing out that when a woman artist exhibits a male nude, 'she will seem to be flaunting her immorality, while inviting the reader to join in her intimacy with the model – in our culture an obscene idea.'[148] Thirty years later, I read 'All the Men I Never Married No. 1', a poem that lists ex-partners, of the speaker of the poem using a series of intimate details. When I reach the line 'are you surprised, are you judging me yet?' an audience member shouts 'yes!' (I explore this episode more thoroughly in 'Yes, I Am Judging You' page 28).

At the start of every reading, I say aloud the title of my collection. *All the Men I Never Married.* Usually there is a titter from the audience. There are smiles, sometimes smirks. I tell them about numbering the poems. I say I'm up to 48. There is more laughter. Although obscene may be too strong a word, and 'flaunting my immorality' too dramatic, there is still something surprising, maybe even shocking, in a woman writing poems about men. Something that should remain hidden is being brought out into the open, and some people don't know where to look.

It is an easy way of getting a laugh at the start of the reading, of breaking the tension, but increasingly, I began to feel more and more dishonest. I am provoking a laugh at the audacity of a woman talking about men and desire, but I'm bored of it being audacious.

Rosie Parker, writing about the *Women's Images of Men* exhibition in *Spare Rib*, argued that '[w]hen we use men's bodies to reveal our perspective on society there is perhaps a greater chance that we will be heard – and understood.'[149] I do not want to 'use' a man's body to reveal my perspective, but at times during the writing of this book, it's felt like men's bodies are in the way, that I have to 'look' at them to 'see' clearly. Retallack writes that '[t]he present is, in fact, made out of the residue of the past'[150] and I understand that to write as a woman, from a woman-place, I have to write about, towards and through men. Parker acknowledged in her review of the exhibition that some criticism of it came from feminists who saw an exhibition looking at men as 'wasting energy on men'. Parker did not agree, stating that the exhibition 'shifted power relations' so that 'presented through women's eyes, men can no longer be Man'[151].

Making men central to the gaze of these essays and my collection *All the Men I Never Married* has troubled me. I've wrestled with what it might mean to make men central to the gaze of my writing. Shoshana Felman in *What Does a Woman Want? Reading and Sexual Difference* also explores similar concerns, explaining that some of her writing was prompted by the 'desire to be understood by – and to reach an understanding with a man', asking herself whether this desire betrays the 'feminist perspective and my feminist commitment'[152]. In her essay 'Women and Honour: Some Notes on Lying', Adrienne Rich talks about her sense in Virginia

Woolf's *A Room of One's Own* that Woolf was aware, even whilst delivering the talk to a room full of women at Newnham College and Girton College, that she was being overheard by men.[153]

One of the places Adrienne Rich led me, a desire line I followed was to the poetry of Judy Grahn, one of her contemporaries and a poet Rich much admired. Grahn's 1975 collection *The Work of a Common Woman* contains a sequence 'The Common Woman' which consists of seven portraits of women. Each poem has the name of the woman in the title, and specific details about them. For example, the third is 'Nadine, resting on her neighbor's stoop' whilst the fourth is 'Carol, in the park, chewing on straws.' In an introduction to this sequence, Grahn writes that she wrote these poems because she wanted to read something 'which described regular, everyday women without making us look either superhuman or pathetic.'[154]

After I read these poems, I enthusiastically set out on my own project of writing portraits of women, but quickly ground to a halt. I could not seem to 'see' any women clearly enough to write anything that would eventually become a poem. I turned back to writing about men again. Many of my poems contain something of Judy Grahn's portraits and their desire to capture the everyday habits of a person. Still, I was left troubled by my desire to write about men, until I read the rest of Felman's essay. She writes that eventually she realised the importance of addressing women and de-centering men, and that whilst she is also conscious of being 'overheard', she means to be 'overheard and heard'[155].

Felman asks a series of questions in her book. I carry them with me throughout the writing of these essays. She asks '[w]hom do we write for?' and it is this moment I know I am writing for women. She asks '[w]hom do we wish to be read by?' and this answer I am ashamed of, because I want to be read by women, but there is a small part of me that wants to be read by men, that craves their approval, although this part is becoming less vocal, less insistent. She asks '[w]hom are we afraid to be read by?'[156] and I know the answer to this one as well.

In the poems which explore experiences of sexism, I want to be 'heard' and I am not afraid of being overheard, of the conversations or criticism about the work or my decision to write about sexism. But in the poems which I think of as poems about desire, which could also be called love poems, or poems to failed relationships, or ex-boyfriend poems, I want only to be overheard, especially by men, because I am afraid, though these poems, on the surface, are the least challenging.

I cannot call them love poems, because inherent in the title *All the Men I Never Married* is the implication of a kind of failure. This failure is implicit in the mind of the reader from the first poem, that this 'one' is just one in a series. Sarah Kent writes that if women 'intend, like men, to speak of sexual pleasure publicly through the medium of the male nude they must learn to do so without discomfort, embarrassment, guilt or a sense of disloyalty to their men, and to make images that speak without ambivalence, ambiguity or self-consciousness.'[157]

I read Kent's essay and it gives me courage to start to perform the desire poems, to experiment. The first time I can feel my face heating up and tension in my shoulders. Each time it gets a little easier. At one reading I listen as a male poet tells another female poet that 'she is too pretty to be a poet, all the female poets he knows are ugly.' Is it this that I am afraid of, how women poets can be reduced to their bodies, and how performing poems about desire can invite this to happen? After he says this, the female poet tells the other female poets at the festival. We gather together to warn each other about other men at the festival we must be wary of, and the power of these comments are diluted, held up to the light as ridiculous instead of being carried within us.

I write more poems of desire. I want readers to wonder how much desire one life can hold.

Hannah Love discusses how micro-observation can give

the opportunity to focus 'around an implicit or explicit center: an image, a scene, a thing or event.'[158] I want my poems to do this, to take the material of personal interaction and transform it into social knowledge through what L. Alford calls a 'poetics of desire'. Alford defines a 'poetics of desire' as being characterised by 'inflections of interest and lack'. Her understanding of lack is that it is characterised by 'physical and temporal distance.' She distinguishes between desire and love poetry, arguing that in the poetry of love, the distance is 'less central and greater emphasis is placed on appreciation and enjoyment of the relation of proximity', whereas in desire poems, the relation is 'more dominantly characterised by distance, by not having.'[159]

Alford argues that poems that take place after 'having, of union' are no longer poems of desire, presumably because desire has been fulfilled. However, I would argue that poems that take place afterwards (after sex or after a relationship has ended) can still be poems of desire, and driven by a poetics of desire, but they must contain two things. The first is the 'lack' or 'distance' which is so important to Alford. The second is that the object of the desire must be foregrounded. Alford argues that in the poetry of desire, the 'subject's consciousness of its own standing in relation to the object' is paramount.[160]

After reading about Alford's poetics of desire, I decided to try and write my own poems of desire. I decided to focus on the idea of temporal distance. The temporal distance is an inbuilt resistance to the 'closing of desire's gap,' as Alford terms it. Though many of my poems are written in past tense, they often pull the past into the lyric present. The true 'lack' or 'distance' is not just temporal, but also a distance of understanding between the subject and the one who is looked upon, a distance of understanding about what is really happening.

In 'All the Men I Never Married No. 15' (page 115) I wanted to mesh these distances of time and understanding together. The past tense creates temporal distance and places the text firmly in the mode of Alford's poetics of desire.

Towards the end of the poem, I wanted to pull the lyric past into the lyric present, as well as turning the gaze of the poem directly towards the audience or reader, acknowledging that they are present, that they are watching and listening.

In *Lyric Shame*, Gillian White discusses how the poet Anne Sexton 'exposes' the audience, by 'figuring the lyric audience and foregrounding the lyric addressee'. White expands on this, arguing that this technique serves to remind us that 'lyric is an exchange subject to a poetic culture'. White argues that many reviewers were hostile to Sexton's work because they believed her poems reflected her lived life, which then meant that they felt 'suddenly addressed by, or in the presence of, a historically viable person' which disturbs and dismantles the critic and audiences' traditional role in regard to lyric poetry which was to be the 'unseen overhearer'[161].

This exploration of the space between the 'I' and the 'you' in the poem, and the writer and reader is important in terms of expanding how we think about lyric poetry, and what it is capable of.

I have mentioned elsewhere in this book the importance of Rilke's 'Archaic Torso of Apollo' to me. In 'All the Men I Never Married No.15.' (page 115), Rilke's poem features as a text not known in the past that my poem is trying to reach back to. The 'lack' is one of knowledge, of understanding. The lack is one of reading the right thing. The lack is one of knowing. The lack is of the desired one, who appears only briefly in the text before disappearing again.

My poem directs the gaze of the audience to focus on the poem by Rainer Maria Rilke, and on a specific translation by Stephen Mitchell, with the distinctive translation of 'his gaze, now turned to low'. The gaze of the audience is directed to a poem which in itself is about an encounter with another piece of art. The piece of art in question has no gaze because it is headless, and yet, the Rilke poem is all about looking, and being seen. It fixes its own gaze back on the audience with its final last-minute turn when it tells us 'You must change your life'. Or perhaps it is the speaker telling themselves this. Or the poet telling himself to change his life. The poem tells us 'here there is no place/that does not see you'. It is a poem about being seen, being known, being perceived by art.[162]

A poetics of desire with a gaze that sees one man before moving on to the next subverts expectations and traditional power hierarchies. This is a poetics of desire where none of the endings are explained or clear – where the story of the ending is not elaborated on. A true poetics of desire addresses the complexities of desire, not the path from one desire to another, but the place of desire, the landscape that desire took place in.

In 'All The Men I Never Married No. 35' (page 117) my intention was to write a poem that more clearly fitted the poetics of desire described by Alford, particularly her focus on 'not having'. I decided to experiment with a poem set in the present tense, a poem addressed directly to a 'you' but a poem that was also full of distance, full of not-having, not-happening, of almost-happening. Because of the direct address to the 'you', the audience are placed in the position of 'overhearing', rather than being directly addressed in the poem.

Alford argues that 'there are many poems of not yet having' as well as 'poems of having had' but there are no poems 'situated upon the zero point of having, of union just so'[163]. This is primarily because 'language disappears' at this point. I took this as a direct challenge to try and write a poem situated upon this zero point, to try to teeter on the brink of not-having, to stay 'poised on this edge' (line 20). Again, the gaze as something desired comes into this poem when the speaker says 'and please carry on looking at me in that way, / I feel unclothed when you do, just for you, / though not nude, but naked with you in this space.' I wanted to write about a male gaze that does not objectify, gesturing towards John Berger in *Ways of Seeing* when he writes 'To be naked is to be oneself. To be nude is to be seen naked by others and yet not recognised for oneself.'[164] Being poised on the edge allows the speaker to be 'seen', to 'be oneself'.

The end of the poem is the only place where the 'you' of the poem could feasibly be a direct address to the reader or audience. I wanted the audience to feel implicated by this direct challenge, this instruction not to assume meaning or the significance of symbols or images used in the poem. Both the unseen 'you' and the audience are told 'don't assume I'm the woman in that place.' Instead the *I* is the 'cigarette, burning' and the *you*, both the audience and the unseen 'you' are figured as the city, which is starving. The starving audience, hungry for details, for confessionalism, sensationalism, the starving you, hungry for sex, to move from being 'poised on the edge'.

If you would like to read 'Lyric Variations (1)' turn to page 91.
If you would like to read a poem filled with women, turn to page 26.
If you would like to read 'What Is Between-Us' turn to page 158.

AN ELECTRIC CURRENT:
POEMS OF WILFULNESS

21.

When he tells me I'm not allowed to play with cars
because I'm a girl, I bring his arm up to my mouth
and bite. I'm sent to the Wendy House to pretend

to be good. Blank-faced dolls stare up at me.
Pretend oven filled with plastic fish-fingers.
Pretend windows with flowery curtains

sewn by someone else's mother. Pretend hoover,
pretend washing machine. Pretend teapots
and tea-set. I watch through a gap in the wall

as my teacher sits in her chair, crossing her legs
in the way she told us only yesterday
we should copy. *Be ladylike* she said.

Stop showing your knickers. I'm burning in here
as she calls the class to order, waits for them
to cross their legs and settle. I long to sit

at her feet, listen to all the old stories
of sleeping women who wait to be rescued.
The book is a bird, its wings held tight in her hands.

She bends the cover back so the spine cracks,
balances it on one palm, turns to me and tells me
turn around, at once, face the wall.

6.

That a man approached you in a nightclub.
That you were polite at first, then turned your back.
That he insisted on giving you his number.
That you put it in your pocket.
That you danced with your friend all night.
That he stood and watched.
That you were drinking tequila.
That you licked salt from the back of your hand.
That he was waiting outside.
That he grabbed your arm and spun you round.
That you snapped.
That you've always had a temper.
That you were not afraid.
That you swung your fist and clipped his jaw.
That he kicked you between the legs.
That he shouted *I will end you.*
That you fell to the pavement.
That he tried to kick you again.
That a bouncer came and held him back.
That he shouted *I will end you, I will end you, I will end you.*
That the police were called.
That he vanished into the night.
That you were taken to the station.
That he turned up with his lawyer.
That he turned up with his father.
That you still hadn't sobered up.
That he was smirking.
That it was fresher's week.
That you were in pain.
That it was hard to explain about his number in your pocket.
That now you were afraid.
That you were advised not to press charges.
That you hit him first.
That this all happened many years ago.

That you laugh about it now.
That you say *well, I shouldn't have hit him.*
That I both agree and disagree with this statement
That being our bodies in public is a dangerous thing.
That being in public is a dangerous thing.
That our bodies are dangerous things.

41.

If I'm ever bored of monogamy,
I'll come and find you,
we'll go to bed and do

things we would not do
with any other (I won't name
them here.) I don't blame

you for asking, I blame
you for not asking sooner.
I used to think you were a user.

I thought I knew what a user
was. I thought it was just lust
but you were the best

at some things, the best
that I've known. How we pretended
none of it mattered! It's splendid

to look back on it now, it was splendid
to know you. If I'm ever bored of monogamy
I know who to turn to.

5.

We hated the way you followed us around,
called us your girlfriends, the top of your head

barely reaching our shoulders, and the smell,
not just unwashed skin, the same clothes day after day,

the same trainers with holes in, but something else,
some animal smell I thought was contagious.

You often tried to hold our hands or stroke our hair,
or rest your small white fingers on our legs.

I wasn't sorry for you when we ran away
because you tried to lift our skirts above our waists,

or when the boys held their noses
because you'd peed yourself again.

It was Sports Day when one of the girls
finally snapped and hit you with a rounders bat.

I can still hear the thunk from across the field.
I wasn't sorry, even when you ran past crying.

At the other end of the track, children cheered
as the whistle was blown.

My friend said you'd tried to touch her bra-strap,
that she'd hit you again if she had to.

Brown sacks crumpled on the grass,
spoons from the egg-and-spoon race in a glittering heap,

children moving crab-like across the field
and you already running towards the classroom.

The next day your mother waited in reception.
She never came to parents' evenings or concerts,

yet there she was, hunched over and staring at the floor
while you sat next to her, pale-faced and silent.

I like to imagine I felt sorry for you then,
knowing you had nobody to speak for you about the bat,

your unwashed clothes, your hands,
the way they could not stop touching things.

If you would like to see what is between-us, turn to 'Between Us: A Poetics of Perception' on page 71.

If you would like to read 'Doing Gender' turn to page 135.

If you have ever watched the Goo Goo Dolls singing 'Iris' in the rain, turn to 'To Give an Account of the Self' on page 169.

DOING GENDER

I am thinking about the kind of trouble these poems will get me into, have got me into. I am thinking about Judith Butler, and the binary of man/woman I have set up in these poems. How the numbering of each poem allows each man to march past in their singularity and plurality. Men, plural. And I, constituted in relation to all of them. All the men I did not marry, apart from the one I did, significant in his absence, who is summoned into being at the margin of each of these poems, at the same time as the men I did not marry come into view.

In *Gender Trouble,* Butler contested binary terms like 'man' and 'woman', writing that gender is not something we are, but something we continually do, and that gender is 'the repeated stylization of the body, a set of repeated acts within a highly rigid regulatory frame that congeal over time to produce the appearance of substance, of a natural sort of being.'[165]

Gender as a set of repeated acts. Telling stories about men and desire (plural) is not something women are expected to do. If the performance of gender creates the subject, then a woman admitting to desire in a world where this is not recognised as 'feminine' behaviour is not simply subverting expectations of behaviour, but is perhaps a subversive performance of gender itself that reveals its inherent instability.

At a reading, a man who looks as if he's in his sixties comes up to me and nudges me as if I've known him for years. 'You don't look old enough to have known all those men!' he says and winks. When he says the word *known* he emphasises it, his voice dropping lower. I smile and say 'Well, artistic licence!' and he nods and says 'of course, of course'. I feel suddenly exhausted. I think about knowing, and how we know anything. Did I 'know' any of them? Is this what the whole thing is about, trying to get to know them again?

In my poem 'All The Men I Never Married No. 17'[166] a man states that the speaker could not have written a poem about him 'because only the women in my family/know the real me.' The speaker points out that this is a misunderstanding of 'what a poem is for'. The rest of the poem is a series of intimate details about this man – his eyes are bright 'like crushed flowers left inside a book.' The poem captures him walking towards the speaker in just his jeans, the bones of his hips 'jutting out like two beautiful half-formed wings.' However, despite this succession of recollections, the speaker concludes that 'you were right, I didn't know you, I didn't know you at all.' The implication that now the speaker suddenly 'sees' more clearly and 'knows' the man in a better or at least different way to the way she knew him in the past is only a suggestion or even a ghost of a suggestion. Katherine Angel writes that 'writing is how I experience my experience'[167] and this sense of gaining a deeper understanding of the past and the present for the speaker in the poem ghosts its way through the text.

Butler writes that 'we regularly punish those who fail to do their gender right'[168] and I know that this cuts both ways, that this truth hurts men, women, anyone who identifies as non-binary, the trans community in general. Sometimes it feels as if I am skating across a deep lake of hurt but all I can do now is write about my punishments, my failures, my moments of desire which will reverberate through my life.

The man who nudged me, who told me I was not old enough to have 'known' all of those men – should I have told him I was eleven years old when I was first called 'frigid' because I did not want to kiss a boy in my class, and twelve years old when I was called a 'slut' for agreeing to kiss another? Should I have told him – you are not a twelve year old boy anymore, and I am not that twelve year old girl. Women have always been punished for their sexual histories, but part of the job of being 'woman' or even 'girl' is always to negotiate these categories, to 'give an account of oneself'[169], as Butler puts it in her book of the same name, to have a life that slides between and past these terms, until now, with these poems, in their performance and with these essays.

Throughout this book, I have written about the reactions and responses of audience members. A man in his thirties who told me I looked like 'I don't take any messing'. The man in his sixties talking about 'knowing' men with a nudge and a wink.

When Butler says 'the very terms by which we give an account, by which we make ourselves intelligible to ourselves and to others, are not of our making. They are social in character and they establish social norms...'[170]. I know what she means. Somewhere between my language and the receiving of it, something happens that I am not in control of. My words must be heard through social norms, as if social norms are distorted panes of glass we must peer through before we see/hear anything at all. The social norms that sometimes come into play in the moments following a performance are ones where men find it more comfortable and less scary to relate to me as a body rather than a poet, to take notice of my body rather than the words that I gave to the air between us.

When I give a reading about sexism or female desire on a stage in front of an audience, I am 'doing something with this telling, acting on you in some way. And this telling is also doing something on me, acting on me, in ways that I may well not understand as I go'[171]. Sometimes this telling is uncomfortable or difficult for some of the audience, and someone (usually a man, but not always) approaches me because the telling has done something to them, and they do not like it.

I am engaged in a process of recognition between myself and the audience, but what they recognise might not be the thing I want them to recognise. There is always a 'constitutive loss in the process of recognition, since the "I" is transformed through the act of recognition.'[172] Sometimes I will be transformed from a poet into a female body. Butler writes that 'To be a body, is in some sense, to be deprived of having a full recollection of one's life'[173]. The life that I am telling is not the life they hear.

Sexism and acts of sexism can be seen as part of a gender

performance we place on the body of others as well as our own, which enable performances of masculinity and sexuality. They are ways in which 'a body shows or produces its cultural signification'[174]. If a man does not join in with sexism, he might be considered less of a man. If women are not flattered by compliments, they can be accused of being unfriendly, aggressive, ungrateful, even unfeminine. Sexism is part of the process of reinforcing the ways in which gender has been done for so long, and as Butler points out 'If human existence is always gendered existence, then to stray outside of established gender is in some sense to put one's very existence into question.'[175]

When I 'stray outside of established gender' by standing on stage and reading poems about sexism and female desire, some people feel the need to place me back in my established gender role, to make sure I understand that they see me as a body. Though it is now becoming more acceptable to speak publicly about sexism, assault and rape, speaking out can still lead to punishment, to ridicule, to disbelief. Sexism is a gendered activity. Men are the main performers of it and sexism helps to keep the binary categories of 'man' and 'woman' alive and breathing.

Sarah Salih argues that for Michael Foucault, 'merely speaking about sex was a way of simultaneously producing and controlling it'[176] – is this also true of sexism? When I speak about sexism in a performance, sexism is often produced in the room, like an echo or a call and response to the sexism I have spoken about. When this happens, can I control it or change it, and if I can, how? Can I change it by writing about it, relating it here, in this book, in witnessing it, retelling it?

The book *52 Men*[177] by Louise Wareham Leonard carries out a genre-bending act of literary innovation. In a cross between the prose-poem, memoir and autobiographical fiction, Leonard writes a series of 52 portraits of men she has been in relationships with. She uses the first name of each man, revealing intimate details about herself, the men and her relationships with them. Sometimes these portraits drawn in language are accompanied by an actual photo of the man concerned. The photos, and the names make each of the 52 completely specific, or at least give the appearance of specificity. Whilst being utterly compelling, in some ways they let the reader off the hook. There is no chance of them 'seeing' themselves or their behaviour in the text because they are tied to specific men and particular moments. They are not 52 ways of being a man, but rather 52 reports of how these men were men.

If each of the poems in *All the Men I Never Married* looks at a man and in doing so, says 'This is a man' and then changes its mind and says 'No, this is a man', no, 'this is a man', then the category of man and what it means to be a man becomes shifty and unstable. These poems are not, in fact, looking at men. When we look at anything, 'we are always looking at the relation between things and ourselves.'[178] So often women are seen as in relation to a man as his mother / wife/ daughter / sister. We see this often in discussions around sexism and gender-based violence when people comment 'Imagine how you would feel if this was your daughter', as if it is not just impossible, but unreasonable to expect a man to feel empathy towards a woman unless he can imagine it happening to someone who is related to him. I wanted to use the female gaze to write poems that look at a man in relation to women, which is another thing entirely to looking at a particular man, standing alone.

If you have ever been objectified, turn to 'The Body is the Blindspot of Speech' on page 145.

If you have ever objectified someone, turn to 'The Body is the Blindspot of Speech' on page 145.

If you would like to think about desire, please turn to 'Poems of Desire: A Mode of Attention' turn to page 114.

INTIMATE WITNESS:
A POETICS OF WATCHING

45.

Remember that night we'd been out drinking
and on the way home heard raised voices,

saw a couple across the road, arguing, leaning
towards each other and then he slapped her,

once across the face, then turned and walked away.
She stood there for a while and then she followed,

down Rawlinson Street as the lights from passing cars
fell on her, then swept on by. We didn't call out

or phone the police. We didn't speak, not to her
or him or to each other. When we got home

we didn't talk about the woman in the denim skirt,
holding her white shoes by the straps.

It's not possible I saw her feet, yet I remember them,
the blackened soles from walking on the pavement,

the sore on the heel where the strap had rubbed
and raised a patch of red. We did not speak to her

and so we made her disappear, limping into the night,
trying to keep up with that man, who knew she'd follow

so did not turn around, hands thrust into his jeans,
front door key hot between his fingers.

43.

When I open my ribs a dragon flies out
and when I open my mouth a sheep trots out
and when I open my eyes silverfish crawl out
and make for a place that's not mine.

When I open my fists two skylarks soar out
and when I open my legs a horse gallops out
and when I open my heart a wolf slips out
and watches from beneath the trees.

When I open my arms a hare jumps out
and when I show you my wrists a shadow cries out
and when I fall to my knees
a tiger stalks out and will not answer to me.

Now that the beasts that lived in my chest
have turned tail and fled, now that I'm open
and the sky has come in and left me
with nothing but space, now that I'm ready

to lie like a cross and wait for the ghost
of him to float clear away, will my wild things
come back, will the horse of my legs
and the dragon of my ribs, and the gentle sheep

which lived in my throat and the silverfish
of my eyes and the skylarks of my hands
and the wolf of my heart, will they all come back
and live here again, now that he's left,

now I've said the word whisper it rape,
now I've said the word whisper it shame,
will my true ones, my wild, my truth,
will my wild come back to me again?

23.

It didn't really help, the story of Othello and Desdemona
and Iago and poison in the ear and though our teacher

taught us about poor Desdemona, bad Iago, Othello escaped
almost blame free, possessed by jealousy, driven into a state

so when my ex became my stalker all the boys in class
        ignored me
and every lesson he looked through me until the evenings
        when he

was drunk and in a nightclub and then he'd ring and start
        to cry
and try to find out where I was or where I'd been, asking
        why

I wouldn't listen, why I'd stopped picking up the phone.
Sometimes I answered it with silence, imagined him alone

listening to my nothing. That year of A-Levels, I got myself
        a stalker
and the police said *aren't you flattered?* In the station there
        was laughter

at the forty phone calls every day for weeks. He said that I'd
        agreed to
be with him forever, and then I'd changed my mind, what
        could he do

but become my stalker and wait till darkness fell and slash
        my father's tyres
or call fire engines to my house though there was nothing
        catching fire.

When my ex became my stalker, he convinced my mum to
    let him in
then locked himself inside the bathroom. It felt like I'd let
    him win

even though it finished with him in a police cell because of
    texts
he'd sent with threats and words like *kill* and *guess what*
    happens next

and so the police kept him overnight to think about his
    actions
and rang his mother who had no idea how any of this
    happened.

16.

When you rewind what happened, your fist
moving away from my face, your arm pulling back,
tracing a half moon in the air, do you watch yourself
running backwards from the flat,
that moment and all of its violence unfrozen,
do you imagine me rising from the bed,
the look on my face before I answer the door?
Do your words return and push themselves back
into your mouth, are you forced to swallow them
again and again? Not *sorry* but you *fucking bitch*,
those words and ones like them, finally lifting from my skin.

I know the living can haunt the living without trying.
Slag. Slut. If I imagine our lives in reverse,
my eyes are always lifting from the floor,
good things are happening. Are you watching
as I vanish into the last gasp of a bus,
reversing through the city? Sometimes I imagine
seeing you again, back row of chairs at an event,
your arms folded, listening to me read
about transformation and violence and loss.
You cannot touch me when I'm speaking,
though what I'm speaking about is us.

If you would like to consider men, please turn to 'Considering Men' on page 164.
If you have a biography of violence, turn to 'Insidious Trauma: A Biography of Violence' on page 100.
If you are interested in the female gaze, turn to 'Women's Images of Men: Desire, Vulnerability and the Gaze' on page 119.

THE BODY IS THE
BLINDSPOT OF SPEECH

Judith Butler wrote that '[i]n speaking, the act that the body is performing is never fully understood; the body is the blindspot of speech'.[179] At one time, I thought this was one of the most beautiful sentences I'd ever read. It was as if I could feel it hovering between two languages, two territories, two ways of being – academic and lyric.

When I first read Butler's sentence, I thought of my driving instructor telling me to 'check my blindspot' before pulling out into the road, of the way I used to move my head in the right direction, but was too panicked to 'see' clearly. I thought of a blindspot as a place of danger, where harm can occur if not checked, if not noticed. I thought of the blindspot as less about seeing, and more about the refusal to notice. I thought of the blindspot as what we choose to look at or look away from.

In a general discussion about ableist language, I asked one of my disabled friends about the word 'blindspot'. They pointed out that it's now considered to be ableist language, because it can usually be substituted for an alternative phrase – 'a weak spot' or 'lack of knowledge'. My friend tells me that the term 'blindspot' is usually used perjoratively, to mean weakness or lacking in ability.

These suggested alternatives do not work in the context of the quote from Butler. The body is not a 'weak spot' or a place where there is a 'lack of knowledge'. The body is the 'blindspot' of speech – a part of speech that cannot be controlled or predicted by language, a place of power, a place that can never be fully understood.

I decide to leave the term 'blindspot' here, though it remains a place of discomfort for me, a term I keep worrying at, and turning over and over.

I'm thinking again of that summer when a poet told me she enjoyed my reading, and then said 'I'm sure you know exactly what you're doing. Reading poems about men with your legs out.' I know what I said in that reading and could list the poems I'd read, but I didn't know what my body was doing, what my body was saying whilst I was speaking. It was saying *something*, all on its own. If the body is the blind spot of speech (if the body is the place-that-cannot-be-contained-controlled-by-language), I do not know what it whispers. What do I say with my body when I'm performing? When I read poems about sexism, what does my body say about sexism? When I read poems about female desire, what does my body say about female desire?

And why did her words make me panic so much? It's taken me years to even start to unpick this. What I understand now by her words was that she believes that I wanted reactions from men, whether that is to seduce them, or merely titillate them. Maybe she meant that I want them to desire me, and my bare legs somehow proved she was right. My body was saying something, was telling the real truth, even whilst my words and my personhood denied this.

In *Tomorrow Sex Will Be Good Again,* Katherine Angel points out that her previous writing about sex and desire would have been used against her in a court room if she was ever raped or sexually assaulted. She says 'I, for my part, had to work hard to keep at bay the knowledge that pulsated under all these responses; that writing publicly about my sexuality could, until the day I die, be used as evidence against me.'[180] Is this what caused my panic, my unease? Not only was I standing and reading poems about men (plural) but I was thoughtlessly doing this whilst wearing a skirt, a double weight of evidence to be used against me if anything happened.

When I was a teenager, I used to walk with a group of friends into town, wearing the shortest skirts we could find, and counting how many times cars full of men beeped at us. We thought it was funny, though we never thought about climbing into the cars that crawled next to us, we did not want to be 'picked up', we only wanted to be looked at, because that was the power we had discovered how to use, and it rested in our long legs, in our barely-there breasts. Even back then, I knew that the power of the gazed-upon was dangerous, unpredictable, not fully in our control. Those long Saturday afternoons as a teenager it felt like everything and nothing was possible. I knew back then that wearing a skirt meant we would be looked at. How could I have forgotten all of that in my thirties, my forties?

I am exploring a different kind of looking now. The desire I am exploring in this book is rooted in the past, a desire that has already both lived and died. The reader knows this because of the title of the book, the title of each poem and the use of numbers to differentiate between them. The relentless marching on of numbers and the unspoken promise that there will always be one more.

In *A Lover's Discourse,* Barthes writes that 'the love which is over and done with in each poem passes into another world like a ship into space.'[181] In *All the Men I Never Married,* the love that is over and done with in each poem passes into the white space between the poems, and moving from one poem to the other, moving from one relationship to the other, is like acceding to 'another logic'[182].

Barthes argues that '[h]istorically, the discourse of absence is carried on by the Woman: Woman is sedentary, Man hunts, journeys; Woman is faithful (she waits), Man is fickle (he sails away, he cruises).'[183] It's easy to think of examples from literature – Penelope waiting for Odysseus to return, Sleeping Beauty not only waiting for the Prince to find her, but waiting in sleep, completely cut off from the world. However, throughout the poems in *All the Men I Never Married,* including the ones contained within this book, the opposite is happening. The female gaze is always moving, always searching. It finds what it's looking for, what it must gaze at. It gives this its full attention, and then stops looking and moves on to the next man, the next relationship, the next 'between-us'[184].

I am speaking about sexism, and maybe my body tells of desire. I am speaking about desire, and maybe my body calls sexism into the room.

If absence can become an 'active practice'[185], by speaking about desire that has passed, which is in the past, by using language to tell about desire, I am manipulating absence. By addressing the men in these poems through the use of the pronoun 'you' they are both absent and present. They are here because they are being addressed, but they are also absent in that they are nowhere to be found, except in language.

When Barthes writes '[w]hat I hide by my language, my body utters'[186] he is talking about hiding his passion, his desire. I am doing one thing with my language, and one thing with my body. The woman who said 'I'm sure you know exactly what you're doing' was certain of this. She smiled when she said it.

A perlocutionary act is the effect of an utterance on some-one else – for example persuading or scaring somebody, but these effects can be intended or unintended. If I think my body is saying 'I am here' by taking up space, but really it is saying something else, then does this make the body an utterance, and this response ('I'm sure you know what you're doing. Reading poems about men with your legs out') a perlocutionary act?

I speak about sexism and a perlocutionary act is produced, and sometimes it is not the effect I intended. I speak about female desire and a perlocutionary act is produced and I do not know what it will be. The body is the blindspot of speech (or the body-is-the-place-of-other-knowledge) and its effects are never fully understood. Parts of the body (like bare legs) become sexual signifiers, and when your body is a sexual sig-nifier, the assumption is always that this is deliberate, that you know what you're doing. The body exists, and what it performs depends both on the person whose body it is, but also on the audience that projects certain meaning on the body.

If the body is the blindspot of speech (if the body is the wildness of speech) I know nothing and everything about what it says. When Butler writes that the body is 'sustained and threatened through modes of address'[187], it is my body and yours she is talking of, and though Butler is talking about address in conversation, I think these ideas can be translated across to how address works in poetry.

In the performance space, the bodies of audiences and readers can be both sustained and threatened by poetry that addresses them directly, that asks them a question, such as in 'All the Men I Never Married No. 1' with the line 'are you judging me yet, are you surprised?'[188], or poetry that asks them to imagine, such as 'All the Men I Never Married No. 7' (page 41) with the first line that asks the audience to 'Imagine you're me, you're fifteen'. Audiences can be both sustained and threatened by poetry that asks them to empathise, to feel, or that ignores them entirely and talks to someone else. When Butler writes that by addressing another, we expose the body of the other as 'vulnerable to address'[189] then the possibility of understanding something about power, who has it and who does not is revealed.

The body is the blindspot of speech, (the blindspot as another language) yet often it is the body that speaks when language fails. In 'All the Men I Married No. 4' (page 43) the sea of white space allows the poem to sway down the page, reflecting the content of the poem and the speaker's intoxication. I use white space here, also, to indicate changes of location and the passage of time: 'first I was there / now I'm here / on the bed / on my back' as well as the movement of inanimate objects: 'the staircase bending / and swaying'. Later I use white space in the middle of lines when one body overpowers the other, creating a visual gap between the two bodies that is not there in the image created by the poem:

> your knees   on my wrists
> your hands   on my shoulders

In 'Projective Verse', Charles Olson writes that

the poet has the stave and the bar a musician has had…he
can, without the conventions of rime and meter, record the
listening he has done to his own speech and by that one act
indicate how he would want any reader, silently or otherwise,
to voice his work.[190]

Voicing is particularly important in 'No. 4', though it is a poem
about being silenced, about having power taken away, another
poem where it is the body that speaks. I needed the white space
to fragment the voice of the poem, to indicate the type of
speech that can be used to describe moments of trauma:

> but my body
>
>   my body asks nothing
>
>   just whispers
>
>   see
>
> I did not let you down I did not
>
> let you down I did not let you down.[191]

In 'All The Men I Never Married No. 13' (page 39) the taxi
driver tells the speaker to 'relax, just relax', even though the
speaker has not communicated verbally that she's
frightened. The body communicates in place of language. It
is the arm that 'flings open the door before I give it per-
mission.' The body as the place where consciousness
happens. The speaker in this poem knows they are in a
dangerous situation yet tries to pretend all is normal. The
rules of polite society bind her much more tightly than the
man she is in a car with, but her body will not be bound by
these rules or expectations.

The unruly arm with a mind of its own recalls 'The Wilful
Child', a fairy tale explored at length in Sara Ahmed's *Living
a Feminist Life,* but originally a Grimm's fairy tale. In the
original, the gender of the child is not made explicit, but
Ahmed explores a version of the story with the child as a wilful
girl who will not do as she is told. Eventually God allows her
to become ill to punish her because she is wilful, and she dies.

Even in death, her arm rises from the grave, and her mother takes a rod and beats the arm until it is still.[192]

In 'All the Men I Never Married No 13' (page 39) wilfulness is figured as silent resistance, as running away, as moving away, as removing the self from the situation. When this wilfulness, this resistance shows itself, the speaker is told to 'relax'. Ahmed tell us that '[w]hen we are not willing to participate in sexist culture, we are wilful.'[193] The body of the speaker is not willing to sit in the car a moment longer than necessary, even while the speaker is willing to placate and pacify the driver by giving him a tip.

The body as wilful. The arm as wilful, though the speaker is not, though the speaker is silent and does not speak up. The arm as the active agent that 'flings open the door'. The leg, not a bare leg this time, but a leg with a will of its own which 'finds the pavement before I can think.' In this poem, the ground may not be in the expected place. In this poem, it is possible to be both wilful, and willing. To resist and to comply.

Ahmed points out that the story of the wilful girl is addressed to a 'willing girl'[194] who does not appear in the text. The willing girl is the reader of this story, this warning is for her. I do not want to address my poem to a willing girl or a willing woman. I do not want it to be a warning about what can happen to you as a woman, just by getting in a taxi, just by going to work, or returning home. It cannot be a warning because situations like this are already happening and have happened, and will continue to happen. Can a poem be a call to be wilful, to allow the body to be wilful, to know what it knows and act upon it?

Maybe there is no such thing as a 'wilful' woman / girl or a 'willing' woman / girl. In real life, we are all composites of both of these figures and we move between the two of them consciously and unconsciously. I want my poems to address the wilful / willing woman and call her to attention. I want the call to wilfulness / willingness to be a call both to the body and to language.

I also want to address those men who are part of this story. As Ahmed points out, '[s]o often people do not recognise their actions as violent'[195]. By placing the space of a poem around the re-telling of this incident, by using the female gaze to generate empathy, I hope that this poem addresses men too and at least opens a space to allow them to reflect on their own actions and reactions in a society where sexism is normalized.

The story of the wilful girl, and Ahmed's discussion around wilfulness helped me to come to terms with my own complicity in the incidents explored in the poem. Virginia Woolf called for 'a room of one's own' for women in the fight for feminism and independence. Ahmed gestures to this essay in her discussion of wilfulness as situated in the body as well as in language, but goes further, arguing that not only do we need a room of one's own, we also need to acquire 'a will of one's own'[196]. Ahmed argues that wilfulness will then be an 'electric current' that can 'pass through each of us, switching us on'[197].

If your body has ever been wilful, turn to 'An Electric Current: Poems of Wilfulness' on page 129.

If you would like to consider what is between-us, turn to 'Between-Us: A Poetics of Perception' on page 71.

46.

I let a man into my room because I couldn't bear
the thought of him with someone else.
Even though he wasn't, never had been,
never would be mine. I showed a man
into my room as if I was selling him the space.
I opened the door and let a shadow
follow me inside. I didn't turn on the light.
I turned on every light. I allowed a man
into my room and he was kind.
I let a man follow me to my room
and didn't close the door in time.
I let a man push past me through the door
and told myself I didn't really mind.
I let a man into my room which turned
into a lift and we were together then apart
then together then apart depending on
whether the door was open wide.
I let a man into my body and let him sleep
inside my room. I let him in, I let him in,
I said that he could do those things
but only in my mind. I let a man
into my room and took a vow of silence,
took a vow of there's no turning back,
because a mind is not for changing.
The men inside my room do not like leaving.
They think they know my name
but one of us is lying. I step across
the threshold. I follow them inside.
Once they're in, they're in.
I open then I close my eyes.

Turn to page 154 to read 'The Annihilation of Men'

THE ANNIHILATION OF MEN

In 2020, 'All the Men I Never Married No. 46' (page 153) was published in *The New Statesman* under the title 'I Let A Man'. Shortly afterwards, I was tagged in a tweet by a male poet who said that the poem objectified men. Later, a letter by the same man was published in the Readers section of *The New Statesman*:

> It is part of a growing liberal backlash against men, seeking to denigrate and reduce them at every turn. Take Moore's stance to its extreme conclusion – which is being echoed in many ways and through many platforms and it will result in the annihilation of men, as outlined in V. Solanas's *The Scum Manifesto*.

I began to think about the word 'objectification' which kept coming up in the exchanges between myself and the male poet, and his exchanges with other Twitter users. It's not the first time a man has accused me of objectifying men in a poem, although it is the first time that accusation was levelled at this particular poem. I wonder if this man knows what objectification means. I wonder if I know what objectifying means. I start to doubt myself, to doubt the poem.

In her article 'Objectification', Martha C. Nussbaum writes that at the heart of objectification is the act of treating a human being as an object. Nussbaum identifies seven different ways of objectifying a human being:

1. Instrumentality: The objectifier treats the object as a tool of his or her purposes.
2. Denial of autonomy: The objectifier treats the object as lacking in autonomy and self-determination.
3. Inertness: The objectifier treats the object as lacking in agency, and perhaps also in activity.
4. Fungibility: The objectifier treats the object as interchangeable (a) with other objects of the same type, and/or (b)

with objects of other types.

5. Violability: The objectifier treats the object as lacking in boundary-integrity, as something that it is permissible to break up, smash, break into.

6. Ownership: The objectifier treats the object as something that is owned by another, can be bought or sold, etc.

7. Denial of subjectivity: The objectifier treats the object as something whose experience and feelings (if any) need not be taken into account.[198]

Nussbaum argues that these seven different ways of objectifying someone can take place in conjunction or in different combinations, or one at a time. It is possible to objectify another without knowing that you are doing so.

I wrote about this incident as part of my PhD research into poetry and sexism, and carried out a line-by-line analysis of my poem to examine if there was any objectification present in the text. My conclusion was that the only objectification I could identify was self-objectification. In the poem, relating to Nussbaum's fifth point about violability. The speaker's lack of boundary integrity permeates the poem in the lack of boundaries around entering or leaving a room.

Back when this all happened, I felt the need to 'prove' that the poem did not objectify men. I wrote 1500 words to justify myself, which became part of my PhD thesis. I don't feel that need now, so I haven't included those 1500 words here. I don't want to keep replicating the extra labour of being a woman and living a creative life. So often our art, our creative process is halted as we take on the work of defending ourselves and the words we've written or the paintings we've painted or the sculptures we've made, from bad faith arguments.

Instead, I would like to talk about the role that poetry can play in examining the complexities of power, control, complicity, consent, victim-blaming and responsibility. These are not problems that can be solved by poetry, but poetry can pose questions about them, and the role they play in our own lives. Poetry can be a way of opening up these words for investigation. Poetry can be a way of examining Irigaray's concept of the 'between-us' between self and other, between writer and reader.

Katherine Angel writes that 'women have no choice but to explore and discover their lives, and indeed their sexuality, in a landscape of sexual violence'[199]. The speaker in my poem moves through a landscape of violence and yet carries on anyway. In some ways, it is the speaker who is the shadow slipping in and out of the room. We never catch sight of her. Her ambivalence, her two-mindedness, her un-decidedness is impossible to control and maybe this is what some male readers find threatening.

Instead of defending the poem against accusations of objectification, or the suggestion that the poem is calling for the annihilation of men, I'd like to talk about the difficulty and complexity of desire. Angel writes that:

> Sex is social, emergent, and responsive; it is a dynamic, a conversation. Our desires emerge in interaction; we don't always know what we want; sometimes we discover things we didn't know we wanted; sometimes we discover what we want, or don't, only in the doing.[200]

This complexity around desire and attempts to discuss it, even in a poem, can be unsettling. Writing poems about the men I never married is not an attempt to talk about women's desire in a vain hope that acknowledging that female desire exists will eventually mean women will stop being shamed for having it. Women will continue to be shamed for not knowing what they want, which has also been described as leading someone on. Worse than this, and at the other end of the spectrum, it's as dangerous for a woman to admit to having desire.[201]

Angel points out that '[e]vidence that a woman has used apps such as Tinder to meet sexual partners can work against her in a courtroom, even if this is irrelevant to the allegation before the court'[202]. Women learn quickly in cases of sexual assault or rape, that any indication that they have felt sexual desire, whether for the accuser or in past relationships can be used as proof that they were willing participants in whatever violent act occurred.

Experiential poetry can describe what it's like to live as a woman in what Angel refers to as a 'landscape of violence.' Whether we like it or not, even consensual sexual encounters take place in this landscape, complete with the rape myths that are repeated in courts, in the media and by the general public.

Men and women live in this landscape together and we are all implicated, impacted and changed by it in different ways. Lyric poetry can hold a space open for a discussion about the complexity of desire. If finding out what we want in terms of desire 'only in the doing'[203] can be talked about in a lyric poem, the next step is to discover how to talk about desire in this way in real life, how to acknowledge that it is, as Angel puts it, a 'conversation' and a 'dynamic.'

If you have been a long time without thinking, turn to 'All The Men I Never Married No. 8 on page 163.

If you feel that men need more consideration, turn to 'Considering Men' on page 164.

If you would like to look at desire, turn to 'Poems of Desire: A Mode of Attention' on page 114.

WHAT IS BETWEEN-US

Luce Irigaray argues for the importance of 'perception', stating that '[c]ultivating perception means being attentive to the qualities of both what is perceived and the one who perceives.'[204] The poems in this book, taken from *All the Men I Never Married,* could be described as a series of portraits of men, but they are also a series of self-portraits. No matter how hard I try, I cannot get away from myself, which insists on being inserted into these poems, alongside the men I am looking at. I am standing next to them, in each type of relationality I describe. I am there in my perception of them, and their perception of me, and the reader's perception of us both.

How can I utilize poetry to ensure that I cultivate perception? How can my poetry ensure I remain attentive to the qualities of what is perceived as well as being present as the one who perceives? When Irigaray asks '[h]ow do we humans share this cradle, this nest, these surroundings?... How do we share the air [...] how is the between-us possible?'[205] I want to answer her with poetry. As a poet, as a writer, I want to write the 'between-us', not the 'I' or the 'you'.

I am writing about the between-us from a distance of years, through the distance of language. There are poems of desire here, and poems of trauma, and poems of violence, and sometimes the poems of desire contain the biggest distance of them all. Inside the poems of desire there is always a kind of failure, or a documenting of the failure to recognise the 'between-us' in the moment of it happening, to be destined to recognise it only when looking back through distance.

Adriana Cavarero explains that '[l]ife cannot be lived like a story, because the story always comes afterwards, it results; it is unforeseeable and uncontrollable, just like life.'[206] We do not know what part of our life becomes the story until later. I am telling you a story, which is also a poem, and what happens next is 'unforeseeable and uncontrollable' and could change both of us. It is only afterwards we can write the 'between-us', only afterwards we can make a story of it, a poem of it, a telling of it.

Throughout *To Be Two* Irigaray calls for the reconceptualization of two human beings as two separate subjects, rather than 'subject' and 'other'. She argues that 'coming to a stop in front of the other is recognition, but it is also a desire and appeal to overcome the interval which separates us.'[207] The poems in this book, and more widely in *All the Men I Never Married* are a way of coming to a stop in front of the other, who may be the subject of the poem, or the reader of the poem, to discover the distance which separated and separates. If these poems are driven by perception, then they will become a 'bridge towards a becoming which is yours, mine and ours'[208] and what I mean by the use of this quote and those pronouns is not just the men contained in these poems, or the versions of them, but the readers of these poems as well, who I hope may also be invited to look, and feel looked at with perception.

One way to ensure that the 'between-us' remains perceptible and present in my poetics is to ensure I activate the female gaze, which always says 'I see you seeing me'[209], rather than the stereotypical male gaze that objectifies, the gaze I've grown up with, the gaze I've read with and consumed art with all my life. Irigaray writes that '[i]n their desire for the other, male philosophers generally evoke sight and touch. Thus, like their hand, their gaze grasps, denudes and captures.'[210] I do not want to reduce the person – whether self or other – to only a body, (mine or another's) to something that can be seen and touched, that can be denuded, grasped or captured, even if these actions are only carried out in language.

In 'All the Men I Never Married No. 1'[211] I list a series of men with a single identifying feature such as 'the one who had an ear infection' or 'the kickboxer with beautiful long brown hair.' I risk reducing them to objects, a paper-thin version of a fully-rounded human being. And yet. I hope they are rescued, I hope the poem is rescued by the insertion of the self, the one who is perceiving – how, in the poem, I sit with the man with the ear infection 'always on his left'. I hope the kickboxer with 'beautiful long brown hair' is rescued from being 'reduced to sensation'[212] by the inclusion of the gesture – his hair 'tied with a band at the nape of his neck'. The nape of the neck as an area of vulnerability. The noticing of this as a moment of tenderness.

The noticing of this without grasping, without capturing. To make the noticing full of moving on, full of letting go, full of refusing possession. The perceiving of these details is not to objectify, but an attempt to describe the 'between-us' in language, to hold with the female gaze both their bodies and their consciousness, and my body and my consciousness.

And to do this and not to 'reduce the other to mere meaning, to my meaning.'[213] To always ask through language 'how do we give each other grace, how do we see each other, the one in the other?'[214] And to do this and find that one way of perceiving is that the female gaze could transform into the glimpse, as the other moves into the line of sight and then away again, or the glance – the other seen from the corner of the eye, a sideways look, which is quick enough for understanding, quick enough for perception, fleeting enough for grace.

To hold in my consciousness the difference between nude and naked. To be naked is 'to be oneself'[215]. I am talking about the bones of his hips, 'jutting from his jeans like two beautiful half-formed wings'[216]. Our bodies together 'like two unlit candles'[217]. To perceive that to be nude is 'to be seen naked by others and yet not recognised for oneself.'[218] To always recognise these men as selves. As a self. As themselves.

In 'All the Men I Never Married No. 35' (page 117) the speaker of the poem acknowledges the gaze of the other:

> and please carry on looking at me in that way,
> I feel unclothed when you do, just for you,
>
> though not nude, but naked with you in this space.

but this is not the male gaze, where the woman is 'displayed as sexual object'[219]. This is a different type of gaze, one in which the looked-at also takes part in. In this poem, both speaker and addressee are looking at each other, and they are both 'naked', rather than nude.

In 'All the Men I Never Married No. 22' (page 73) the gaze of the poem comes to rest on the 'last night' between two lovers who try to articulate what is between them. The desire between them can be seen from the start of the poem. It begins in the dark, with the body of the speaker 'turning under your hands'. The suggestion by the unnamed 'you' of 'let's go back to bed' tells us that this is where they have been already. There is intimacy, knowledge of each other's bodies. The speaker traces the 'outline of your bones' and the 'you' of the poem is described as 'heat and blood and fingers and chest.'

This apparent reduction of the other to a series of body parts is always in an attempt to perceive, to understand the other. The gaze of the poem continually circles back to the failure of the speaker to truly 'know' the other, and the realization that the knowing of the other cannot be achieved solely through the body, or through desire. It becomes apparent that the other transforms to someone unknowable when they get dressed and enter the outside world. There is a strangeness attached to the everyday actions of doing washing or ironing implied in the act of remarking on them. When other people are around nobody recognizes the 'between-us' between them. The speaker says 'I ran with you / in the wind and rain, on the track or the beach / and nobody knew we went home together.'

The poem is infused with the failure to not know the other, containing a series of questions addressed to the other that remain unanswered appearing towards the end of the poem, in contrast to the earlier intimacy portrayed. The last sentence explores the space that existed between them and asks how they both managed to 'hold something back'. Irigaray would argue that this holding back is a necessary part of any relationship. She writes '[y]ou who are not and will never be me or mine are and remain you, since I cannot grasp you, understand you, possess you.'[220]

Some of these poems are portraits of men, but all of them are portraits of the between-us, of what was impossible and possible. The between-us I am writing about, I give to you, the reader, in the hope that in turn it conjures up the between-us, between you and I, in the hope that language can be used to describe it.

If you would like to read 'Insidious Trauma: A Biography of Violence' turn to page 100.
If you would like to read 'Between-Us: A Poetics of Perception' turn to page 71.
If you would like to read 'To Give an Account of the Self' turn to page 169.

8.

You must write, and read, as if your life depended on it...
Adrienne Rich

On the train a man asks me what I'm reading.
The mind as an empty and flooded field

He tells me about his job and his wife and his children.
The mind as water rising through green.

He tells me about money and Brexit and immigration.
The mind as a tree at the edge of the field.

I put my book away. Repeat. Repeat. I put my book away.
I have been putting my book away all my life.

I put away my hands and my mouth and my eyes.
I have been a long time without thinking.

I can sit here and listen and live without field or water or green.
I have been a long time without thoughts of my own.

Or go back and fold into myself.
White birds with no names.
They row away through the air.

Or enter and drink at the shallow place.
Enter and prepare to be followed.

I am worried about madness and the next sixty seconds.
I put away my heart and the stillness inside.

I smile and say what do you do tell me again and
how many kids do you have remind me again of your wife.

If you would like men to be considered here, turn to 'Considering Men' on page 164.
If you would like women to be considered here, turn to 'Considering Men' on page 164.

CONSIDERING MEN

I am reading Adrienne Rich's *What Is Found There: Notebooks on Poetry and Politics*[221] on the last train home between Manchester and my home town in Cumbria. It's important that it's the last train, that it's a Saturday night, because the last train home has a distinct feel and rhythm to it. At Lancaster, groups of men and women who have been on a night out board the train and converge into one carriage, some still brandishing cans of beer and wine bottles. It sounds like a party is happening on the other side of the sliding doors.

I'm alone until just before the train sets off, when I'm joined by a man wearing what look like chef's trousers. I smile politely as he sits down at my table, and turn the page of my book.

I read the words '[y]ou must write, and read, as if your life depended on it.'[222] I don't get any further than this line because the man in chef's trousers has started to talk. The open book on the table in front of me has not put him off. He tells me he's on his way to Grange, to do a shift at a hotel there, and then he carries on, talking about his work and the number of shifts he has. I'm becoming more and more irritated, but I don't say anything because I don't want to be rude, because I'm on my own in this carriage with him, because there's nowhere to move apart from the carriage with the party. I feel ashamed, and as if a great pressure is building inside me. I cannot stop my eyes falling back to that line. *You must read and write as if your life depended on it.* I think about Adrienne Rich, what she is telling me to do, how I cannot do it, because I cannot ask a man to be quiet.

The man carries on talking. I try and tell myself that he doesn't know I've just read something that is going to change my life. The man tells me he hates train journeys because they are so boring, so he has to talk to pass the time, for entertainment. I know it's not me who he wants to entertain but himself, that he wants someone (something) to pour his words into. I feel as if I'm waking up, as if the world I went to sleep to say the same again.'[229] When I write in 'All the Men I Never Married No.8' 'I put my book away. Repeat. Repeat. I put my book away', and the internal monologue, represented in italics in the poem answers *I have been putting my book away all my life* I am trying to trace the development of this realisation. The first 'I put my book away' is a simple statement of fact. The second holds a realisation about the significance of this act, and the final repetition contains the wider understanding that was reached by writing these words.

There are inherent difficulties in being a woman in a public space such as public transport. How women move through these spaces and claim them as their own, rather than feeling intimidated or as if they are there to entertain/listen to men is a problem that has not been solved, or even fully acknowledged.

Using public transport is both public and private in nature – public in that it is in a public space, and private in that it consists largely of individuals going about their own business. Lyric poetry is also balanced between private and public worlds. Vicki Bertram writes that it is a 'strange hybrid; existing on a crepuscular boundary between private and public worlds, its roots lie in the personal, but it transforms this originary matter, and then offers it up to the world at large.'[230]

This common experience of being a woman on the train and being interrupted and talked 'at' is a private one which takes place in public. It can be transformed through the use of lyric poetry and offered up as an examination of one way in which men and women take up space differently, and how domination can work.

In *On Lies, Secrets and Silence* Rich writes that the 'possibilities that exist between two people, or among a group of people, are a kind of alchemy.'[231] This is something she has explored at length throughout her career, in both her poetry and prose. In many of her poems, possibility is always present, even when impossibility is acknowledged. In her poem 'In the Evening' she writes 'Our minds hover in a famous impasse /

and cling together.'[232] Both minds are considering the impasse, both focused on it, even if they cannot quite move past it. Both 'In the Evening' and 'Trying To Talk With A Man' seem to imply that the answer to these problems can only be found in how we relate and communicate with each other. These poems seem to imply that the answer to these problems can only be found in how we relate and communicate with each other.

What kind of reaction can be set off if the possibilities between men and women are examined and held up to the light, if they are talked about honestly, if women feel safe to say how they really feel? What can happen in the world if when Adrienne Rich tells a woman to 'read and write as if your life depended on it' that woman is free to follow that advice, to live her life by it?

If you would like to read 'Intimate Witness: A Poetics of Watching' turn to page 140.

If you would like to read 'All The Men I Never Married No. 46' turn to page 153.

If you wonder about how some women see some men, turn to 'Women's Images of Men – Desire, Vulnerability and the Gaze' on page 119.

TO GIVE AN ACCOUNT OF THE SELF

A friend sends me a link to a video. It's a band I've only vaguely heard of: *The Goo Goo Dolls*. They are playing on an outside stage in the pouring rain. The lead singer's hair is plastered against his face, and his black shirt, half undone, clings to his chest and stomach. I find out later the song is called *Iris*, although this word is never mentioned in the lyrics. At one point, in the bridge, while the guitarist plays a solo, the singer turns to the camera man and tells him to turn the camera so we can see the crowd. They stretch far into the distance, and though there are only a few umbrellas dotted here and there, the crowd don't seem to mind or even notice the torrential rain. And it is torrential, the type of rain where, if you have a warm house you can return to, there is nothing to do but laugh about it, no way of even trying to stay dry, the type of rain that can invigorate you.

Copyright rules make it impossible to quote it here directly, but there is a lyric that returns throughout this song in which the singer pleads to be known by another person (the 'you') for who they are. This reminds me of Barthes, and Butler and Irigaray. The line is not an insult or a slur, but the desperate desire of it calls up a kind of pain in me. It is the same desire that Roland Barthes articulates in *A Lover's Discourse* when he writes 'I want to understand myself, to make myself understood, make myself known, be embraced; I want someone to take me with him.'[233] If you watch the video and listen to the song, you will know the line I mean.[234]

The 'you' that the singer addresses in this song, as he holds the microphone out to the audience who sing the lines back to him, seems to be both the unseen lover and the audience. What does this mean in light of what Irigaray says about unknowing, when she insists '[w]e can remain together if you do not become entirely perceptible to me, if a part of you stays in the night.'[235] Now, I am singing along with Irigray, I am singing along with Barthes, I am singing along with *The Goo Goo Dolls*.

Is it possible to want someone to know who you are without possessing them? The never-ending desire of it. I know that '[t]he more one seeks oneself in language, the more one loses oneself precisely there where one is sought.'[236] I understand this. The song, the poem, the sentence as beautiful failure, as always falling short. I cannot explain what happens between the space of one poem and another, how the self that is present in one poem transforms and becomes the self that is present in the next.

In each of the poems in *All the Men I Never Married*, men and their actions are placed at the centre of the poetic gaze. The relationality between the men and the speaker of the poem is traced and in turn this traces a relationality between the speaker and the audience, between the writer and the reader.

If I am telling you (in a poem) that I want 'you' to know me in some way, then it is on the pronoun 'you' that the text falters. The 'you' can be both the self (I want to know who I am) or the audience or reader (I want you, or I want all of you to know who I am) or the 'you' could refer to the man that the poetic gaze is focused on (I want him to know who I am). The man in each of the poems in *All the Men I Never Married* is both a man, and a cipher or a symbol of a man, a man that never existed, or an Everyman.

It's not just the pronoun 'you' that creates unstable ground in a text. According to Judith Butler, 'when the 'I' seeks to give an account of itself, an account that must include the conditions of its own emergence, it must, as a matter of necessity, become a social theorist.'[237] When I give an account of sexism, I realise that the conditions for my own passivity, my own acceptance are threads linking me to the social world, linking me to what has come before.

In 'All the Men I Never Married No. 21' (page 129) I've tried to demonstrate what Butler is referring to when she argues for the need of the 'I' to become a 'social theorist' when giving an account of itself. One day when I was still a music teacher, still working in schools, I stood and said nothing as the class teacher told a seven year old girl to 'close her legs.' I was hit by a wave of recognition when I heard those words and saw the blush on the child's face, but I was also lost for words. It brought back to my awareness early memories of sexism.

I'm thinking again of Virginia Woolf's 'moments of being'. Woolf never really provides a comprehensive definition of what a 'moment of being' is, describing them variously as both a 'sudden violent shock' and as moments that 'come to the surface unexpectedly'. She also intimates that a moment of being may hold the potential for insight, discovery or even epiphany[238], In that sense, I understand them as not just vivid memories, but moments when we are fully conscious in the world – a moment where we have shaken off any false consciousness, where sometimes we can glimpse a wider pattern at work around us or inside us.

The pattern revealed to me as I wrote 'All the Men I Never Married No. 21'(page 129) and remembered both the anger at injustice and the consequent shame of losing my temper was complex. I didn't realise all the things I learnt in that moment, and moments like it. I didn't know I'd absorbed them until I wrote the poem. I learnt that there are certain things girls cannot do, such as playing with 'boys toys' or retaliating with violence, that girls should not have anger or tempers at all, that girls should not take up too much space, that a girl's body is a sexual thing, and the girl is responsible for this, that 'girls toys' are not as desired as 'boys toys' and in fact can be used as a space for punishment, that girls in stories spend their time sleeping or waiting to be rescued, and finally that women are not only complicit but play an active role in these injustices.

The account given in this poem of an early experience of sexism links to other more traumatic and serious encounters merely by being placed in a poem alongside other poetic treatments of this subject. The white space which surrounds these encounters both separates and links them together.

I am thinking of the song again, and the lyric about wanting to be known, the desire it articulates. I want to give an account of myself and an account of oneself is 'always given to another, whether conjured or existing'[239]. Performing these poems has situated me at the border of what I know and do not know. It has forced me to confront what it is like to

> continue in a dialogue where no common ground can be assumed, where one is as it were, at the limits of what one knows yet still under the demand to offer and receive acknowledgment to someone else who is there to be addressed and whose address is there to be received.[240]

I'm at a reading, where I'll be performing two sets. I read 'All the Men I Never Married No. 13' (page 39) which examines an experience of sexism with a taxi driver and the speaker of the poem's conscious and unconscious reactions to it. In the interval, a woman comes up to me and asks 'Haven't you got any poems where women fight back? If a man put his hand on my leg on public transport, I would just say No! very loudly!'. I reply that her response is coming dangerously close to victim-blaming, and she shakes her head, holds up her hands, and says 'oh no, I would never, ever do that!'

I can't remember what happened next, although it did not feel as if we reached an understanding. I think about Adrienne Rich's line from 'In the Evening' – 'our minds hover together in a famous impasse.'[241] I think my mind is hovering above the impasse – but where is hers? Is it waiting there too, unnoticed by me, or did it sail straight over, refusing to look down, or around, or behind? Did the conversation shift anything inside her in the same way I felt something shift inside me when she asked that question?

When I get on stage for the second set, I say that somebody has asked if I have any poems about women fighting back, and then I read 'All the Men I Never Married No. 21' (page 129) which is not about a woman fighting back, but about a girl lashing out, and what happens to her, and how the body is used to shame and control her, and how space is used to shame and control her.

I am singing the song again but I write out the words 'I want to give an account of myself.' I conjure up Judith Butler instead of a rock band singing in torrential rain. There is a link between the girl sitting in the Wendy house and burning inside ('All the Men I Never Married No. 21', page 129) and the silent woman sitting in the taxi, ('All the Men I Never Married No. 13', page 39) letting men say the things men say.

This link is what happened to me in my twenties, which I wrote about in a sequence of poems in my first collection *The Art of Falling*[242]. In this sequence I use a fragmented narrative and themes of transformation to examine domestic violence (I also discuss this in 'Desire Lines: An Introduction' page 10).

I want to give an account of myself and I am talking to myself and to you.

The sequence in *The Art of Falling* was my attempt at making sense of those 'moments of being', which were often all I could remember. They remain isolated in my memory, bright painful spots of time surrounded by darkness, by no memory at all. I used to panic that I couldn't remember things chronologically. Through writing those poems, I realised the darkness, the fragmented memory, and even those moments of being are all spells of protection, that my mind was saving me in the only way it knew how.

In contrast to this, it took writing this book to begin to understand that many of the poems in *All the Men I Never Married*, and indeed the essays contained here are a way of accounting for myself. I might have started off trying to account for myself to others, but underneath that, running deeper and more true and more urgent, is a desire to account for myself *to myself*. I want to understand how I, how anyone ends up in a violent relationship, how we survive, how we resist, how we capitulate.

Butler says that for Nietzsche, 'accountability follows only upon an accusation'[243]. The accusation comes from both myself, and also a wider society that still asks why women 'don't just leave', discounting that the time of leaving a violent relationship is the most dangerous time. Why didn't I just leave? The poems in *All the Men I Never Married* are trying to answer this question, from a place of not-knowing, to describe how women move through the world and how conditions for tolerating violence and trauma are created.

Female poets in the UK such as Pascale Petit, Helen Ivory, Fiona Benson and Moniza Alvi have utilized techniques such as surrealism or deployed myth and folk tales to explore and make sense of feminine existence as a 'traumatised exist-ence'[244]. However, there is a silence in lyric poetry around the wider spectrum of gender-based violence and micro-aggression, which is only recently beginning to be broken with the publication of anthologies such as *#MeToo*, published by Fair Acre Press in 2019.

Two contrasting theories of lyric poetry that are dominant in both academic and poetic discourse are relevant here. The first has its roots in Romantic poetry and in particular William Wordsworth and his often-quoted assertion that lyric poetry is the 'spontaneous overflow of powerful emotion.'[245] The second has its origins in the New Critics assertion that lyric poetry is an expression of a persona rather than the poet. Both of these viewpoints based around a humanistic rationale fail to take into account the long history of the lyric which has its ancient roots in epideictic discourse – discourse used to praise or persuade. Lyric poetry can be used to start a conversation about female desire, sexism and its effects on both the individual and society, connecting with its history of being epideictic discourse – 'discourse about meaning and value'[246].

Judith Butler points out the danger of trusting the 'seamlessness of the story' and that the truth may exist in 'moments of interruption, stoppage, open-endedness'[247], and this is exactly why poetry is an ideal vehicle for examining these subjects. The truth about sexism and desire is dynamic, mobile and shifting, and poetry is an ideal form to contain and open up these questions, rather than providing answers.

In the performing of these poems, the limits of what I know are contained within the poems themselves, as I try to articulate the relationality between my self and an other, and allow this to be framed by the relationality between my self and an audience. As Butler points out: '[m]y account of myself is partial, haunted by that for which I can devise no definite story.'[248] Publishing and performing these poems has allowed me to experience this partiality and to understand that an account of the self through poetry only reaches its completion in the reception of the work by an audience or reader. Often my understanding of my own experience of sexism only arrives through the writing of the poem.

Butler's ideas around the importance of change to both the addressee and the speaker in the act of giving an account are relevant here. She writes '[a]nd this telling is doing something to me, acting on me, in ways that I may well not understand as I go.'[249] The 'telling' which takes place in a poetry reading has an effect on both the writer and the audience. It is not possible to predict how our words will be received, and this uncertainty becomes part of the story of sexism, part of the story of female desire.

After a reading in early 2019, I receive the following email from a woman in the audience. She writes:

> I think a dynamic of your work is that it allows for the re-perceiving of earlier experiences, previously cast as shameful (a woman's interpretation) in a gendered social context.
> (personal correspondence, 18 February 2019)

Our exchange leads me back again to Adrienne Rich, and the way she advocated for '[r]e-vision – the act of looking back, of seeing with fresh eyes, of entering an old text from a new critical direction.'[250] Can re-vision also be used when looking back at our own lives? Liz Yorke wrote about Rich's 'lifelong allegiance to poetry (and later, a theory) emerging out of lived experience – the actuality of personal, social and historical experience becomes both "source and resource" for the work.'[251] Can I use re-vision on my own life?

Sometimes I do not have to look back at my old life with fresh eyes. Sometimes I just have to look at my life, the life I am living now. Sometimes I do not even need fresh eyes, I just have to open the eyes I have. Sometimes I just need to awaken. Sometimes I am awake and I behave the same way anyway, and go home and write about it. Sometimes I am awake and I protest about what is happening, with language or silence or my body, with different degrees of success. The goal of writing and performing these poems has shifted in the writing and performing of them. I know that what the singer wants is impossible, that what I want is impossible, that I cannot give an account of myself, yet I cannot stop those words, both Butler's and the line from the song going round and round in my head. I cannot stop singing that song. I cannot stop wanting. Maybe the task of poetry is to 're-vision' our lives, to illuminate what Irigaray calls the 'between-us', the path between you and I as writer and reader, performer and audience, individual and society.

If you would like to be an intimate witness, turn to 'Intimate Witness: Poems of Watching' on page 140.

If you would like to reach a conclusion, turn to 'Variations on a Conclusion' on page 177.

VARIATIONS ON A CONCLUSION

1.

When I try to write this conclusion and am confronted with the blank page, I begin to believe that the years I've spent writing this book are filled with blankness, despite evidence to the contrary, despite the thousands of words I've written that are there waiting to be drawn upon, despite the poems, despite the conversations I've had with other poets, with readers, with audience members, conversations which thread through this book and the thinking which has informed it.

I'm struggling to conclude because sexism does not have a conclusion, and neither does desire. Sexism is a shape-shifter, and so is desire. Sexism is a conversation of sorts, and so is desire. Sexism and desire are always emerging, always in retreat or advancing. It's not in their nature to be still, to not exist. Sexism as something made bigger by denial, and though of course everyday sexism still happens, is happening, to me and around me and despite me, something has changed with this act of putting a poetic frame around it. Something in me has changed in the writing of it.

2.

I am writing this on the 6am train from my home town to Manchester. The guard comes to check my ticket, and tells me to smile. I bare my teeth at him, and sit feeling more and more irritated and angry. I think about all the times over the years that I've been told to smile. At the next station, a man gets on and the guard comes down to check his ticket. I time it perfectly. As the guard turns to walk away, I point at the man. The guard is confused, 'I've just checked his ticket.' 'He's not smiling!' I say loudly. 'Tell him to smile!' I smile encouragingly. The guard is still confused, and doesn't say anything. He walks away down the carriage. I sit smiling to myself.

3.

I conclude that sexism does not mean the thing I thought it meant at the start of this journey. What I meant by sexism at the beginning were encounters I have remembered all my life without thinking about why I remembered them. Stories I considered small not because of their smallness, but because there was a difficulty in saying what they actually were. There was a nothingness at their heart put there by me and by other people. I thought at the beginning of this project that sexism was something I both shrugged off and carried with me, a bag I could not put down, but which did not stop me going about my everyday life. Putting the frame of a lyric poem around these encounters and Jonathan Culler's discussion of the lyric convention of significance helped me to see them more clearly. I began to find it impossible to dismiss or minimise my experiences. The framework of the lyric poem would not allow me to. Using the lyric poem as a structure allowed me to talk about sexism in a way that was impossible in normal social interactions where it's routinely dismissed or minimised. This was an unforeseen and welcome outcome.

4.

My collection *All the Men I Never Married* and the poems from it included in this book have their roots in epideictic discourse – discourse that aims to persuade or praise, discourse about meaning and value. My aim throughout this book was to create a discourse that crosses boundaries between private and public, social and individual, personal and political. I wanted both my poetry and my poetics to move between these boundaries. I wanted this book to be rooted in epideictic discourse, but also to remain open-ended and non-conclusive as a place for transformation both in the writer and the reader.

5.

When I first started writing the essays and poems in this book, I wrote poems of female desire, or love poems because I could not help writing them. At first I thought they were a different project, then I felt relieved because I thought I could use them to 'prove' that I did not hate men. See, I had loved this man, and this man. And this one. And then I learned that female desire often calls sexism to show itself, to come out from where it had hidden its face.

I learned at a conscious level (although I already knew this in my body) that to be a woman and admit to or talk about desire is a dangerous thing. Women understand that whilst it can be risky to say no to sex, it is also inherently dangerous to say yes. As Katherine Angel points out, women know that 'their sexual desire can remove protection from them, and can be invoked as proof – not that violence did not take place, but that violence wasn't wrong *(she wanted it)*.'[252]

So when I write that to talk about desire is a dangerous thing, to write about it, and then to perform it, I mean to use the word dangerous. Still, I did it anyway. I could not help it.

I have raised my own 'critical consciousness'. I know there's still more work to do. I've created a space for transformation of the self, and at the same time I have written about staying silent when confronted with sexism. I have written poems which are at the same time wilful and willing. I have accepted both of these things can exist.

6.

And this has to do with the telling, and the way it acts on you, and the way it acts on me. This has to do with poetry as a way of accounting for oneself, which can only ever be partial.

And this also has to do with the body, and in particular the female body in performance, and how it says things that cannot be controlled. This has to do with your body and mine, and how they can both be sustained and threatened by poetic address.

And this has to do with the between-us, the space that exists that is not you or me, but something made by both of us, something emerging, dynamic, unpredictable, intimate.

CODA: ON WAYS OF LOOKING

/

In the photo, I am standing with eyes glazed, drinking from a bottle of beer.

/

In the photo, I am standing with my best friend, who has a bottle of beer in one hand and a whisky and coke in the other. We are in a nightclub. We are in our twenties. We are not afraid of anything.

/

In the photo, a man stands in the middle of two women. He has his arm around the neck of one, whilst holding a bottle of beer, and his arm around the shoulders of the other. He pulls them both towards himself, closer, closer.

/

In the photo, I am in a nightclub in the time before violence, before I knew its real name, before I followed violence to the flat with the red door.

/

In the photo, I am in the time of who-I-thought-I-was, in the time of dance-all-night, in the time of £1-a-bottle, from sweets-sold-in-nightclubs, in the time of glazed-eyes, in the time of my-body-in-the-grasp-of-another, in the time of who-was-that-fucking-man-anyway.

/

This photo, this photo – I can still smell the whisky and the sweetness of sugar, after all these years, after all this time.

/

In Roland Barthes' *Camera Lucida,* he argues that photographs, or at least the photographs that interest him have something he calls a 'punctum' which he describes as a 'sting, speck, cut, little hole'.

His mother has recently died, and he returns again and again to a photo of her at five years old, although we never get to see that photograph. He says 'For you, it would be nothing but an indifferent picture…but in it, for you, no wound.'[253]

/

I share Barthes' astonishment at the photograph, at its irrepressible ability to testify to what was there, to what existed. Once I existed – the photograph is 'reality in a past state: at once the past and the real.'[254]

/

How that photo takes me back to the Fab Café where the bouncers knew our names and looked after us, bringing us from the back to the front of the queue so we felt chosen and looked after and special and brought us in from the winter streets to the heat of the club brought us in without touching us without expecting anything those men those men with the shoulders and the leather jackets they wanted nothing except our gratitude standing with their arms crossed and the smile that just touches their faces where are they where are they now?

/

Glick writes that benevolent sexism is 'attitudes that are subjectively benevolent but patronising, casting women as wonderful but fragile creatures who ought to be protected and provided for by men[255]. But the girl in the photograph is twenty years away from reading Glick.

/

How the flat with the red door swallowed me whole, how I walked in with violence, not quite arm in arm, not quite following, not quite leading, but I did walk in, not quite with my eyes shut, not quite with my eyes open, it was a strange time, it was a before-time, it was many years ago and I do not remember, except the red door and the way it closed, the way it would not open, or if it did, it opened onto a world that violence also lived in, a world that violence also owned.

/

Outside the flat with the red door, a man at the bus stop follows me to the shop to offer me money to have sex. He follows me back home again. He knows where I live, waits outside at the bus stop and stares at the window. I keep the curtains shut tight, but every time I move them to look outside, he's still there. He's smiling each time I pull the curtain back.

/

Oh but none of these things have happened yet to the girl in the photograph!

/

Ten years after the photograph was taken, I am working in a men's prison, and one prisoner gives me his prisoner number and asks me to write to him, to help him with his poetry, with his song lyrics, and then another prisoner, before I can refuse, tells him to get walking. The first prisoner turns, walks quickly away. The second prisoner apologises and takes the number on the scrap of paper from my hand, before I can say anything. He tells me he will sort this out, that I will not be bothered again.

/

When I was seventeen, two years before the photograph was taken, I am allowed to go to a particular nightclub because my father's friend is the bouncer and he will keep an eye on me, keep me safe. My father takes me there and picks me up again.

/

I have walked under the protection of men. I have walked without the protection of men.

/

My father's friend and the way that he looks at me, and how I use this, to get my friends in the door, especially my friend with the face of a child, who gets turned away everywhere else, especially her, who is kept out of every pub and club, even with her fake ID. My father's friend lets her in with a nod of his head and tells me not to let her go to the bar. I smile and hug him, standing on tiptoe to reach.

/

According to the national charity Refuge, one in four women in the UK will experience domestic violence during their lifetimes, and it often starts with benevolent sexism – a jealous partner will be seen as being protective rather than possessive, or caring rather than controlling, nurturing rather than stifling.

/

Behind the red door is a communal hallway and then stairs leading up but past the stairs is my front door, is our front door, and behind that door is the living room where and the kitchen where and the bedroom where and the garden where

/

I have told you before about Sara Ahmed's 'biography of violence'[256]. I remain interested in what a biography of violence will look like. How one biography of violence can hide another. I think about Kenneth Koch's poem, his one train may hide another, his 'One dog may conceal another/On a lawn, so if you escape the first, you're not necessarily safe.'[257] Behind the experience of domestic violence, behind the red door, behind this biography, lies another biography of violence which led me up the steps, which allowed me to open the door.

/

In the photograph, a man's arm is slung around my shoulders as if he knows me, I am so close I can smell him, and I am bringing a bottle to my mouth as if I like it, as if I'm asking for it.

/

Barthes argues that the *punctum* gives a photograph what he calls a 'blind field'. He argues that a blind field means that any figures in a photograph 'continue living' – they have a whole life external to their captured image.[258] If the punctum in my photograph is that man's arm around my neck, then all of the continuous living the 'I' that is captured in that photograph does, will be done forever with an arm around my/her neck, will be done forever with my face so gently trying to escape just by turning away, an escape without drawing attention to myself/herself.

In the poem 'Monument' by Elizabeth Bishop, the reader is asked to look again and again at the monument, described in painstaking detail. Bishop asks us:

Now can you see the monument? It is of wood
built somewhat like a box. No. Built
like several boxes in descending sizes
one above the other...[259]

The first time I read this poem, I felt as if I was walking
round and round the monument, seeing it from every angle,
without really seeing it at all. If this book could transform into
a single poem, it would be this one. Imagine this text as a
monument. Imagine sexism as a monument. Imagine female
desire as a monument. Now climb inside, crawl underneath,
sit on top and look at the landscape which surrounds them
both, the paths that lead to them, the sightlines, follow the lines
of sight. Imagine this text as a poem.

READER CHECKLIST

ACKNOWLEDGEMENTS

All of these poems can be found in *All the Men I Never Married* (Seren, 2021). Thank you to the editors of the following publications in which some of these poems have appeared: *Agenda, Ambit, MAL Journal, Poem, Poetry Ireland Review, The Dark Horse, The New Humanist, The New Statesman, The North, The Poetry Review, The Rialto, The White Review* and *Wild Court*. No. 47 won the 2021 Ledbury Poetry Competition. No. 40 won third prize in the 2021 *Mslexia* Poetry Competition.

The epigraph for No. 8 comes from *What Is Found There: Notebooks on Poetry and Politics* by Adrienne Rich. No. 15 references 'Archaic Torso of Apollo' by Rainer Maria Rilke, translated by Stephen Mitchel. No. 18 contains a line from Thomas Hardy's poem 'The Voice'. No. 28 contains a line from the song 'I Get Along Without You Very Well' composed by Hoagy Carmichael and performed by Chet Baker amongst others. The first poem 'We Are Coming' is inspired by *The Laugh of the Medusa* by Hélène Cixous.

Thank you to Manchester Metropolitan University for the award of a Vice Chancellor's Bursary whilst conducting my PhD research. I would like to thank my three supervisors – Professor Michael Symmons Roberts for the gift of his careful attention on many of these poems, Dr Angelica Michelis for her unwavering belief and challenge to push myself further, and finally to Dr Nikolai Duffy who gave me permission when I needed it, so that eventually I could give myself permission.

Thank you to Mick Felton at Seren for all of his support, patience and belief in this book and to the rest of the team at Seren. Thank you to Shoshana Olidart who worked with me to edit this book – the opportunity to work with you so closely on this text was such a gift.

Once upon a time I met a wonderful group of women poets in a far-away country and we started talking about what was happening to us instead of pretending nothing was happening, and those conversations and that solidarity changed my life.

Thank you Hilà Lahav, Volya Hapayeva, Linda Klakken and Krystyna Dąbrowska. Thank you to Malika Booker for telling me to get on with this at just the right time and to Helen Mort for teaching me how to be brave. Thank you to Daniel Sluman for your thoughtful conversation about disability and language – I hope this is a conversation we can continue for many years to come. Thank you to my current students at Manchester Metropolitan University who continue to invigorate and inspire my thinking. Martin Kratz was a huge help throughout the writing of my PhD, and this book probably wouldn't exist if he hadn't been there to cry at – thankyou. Some friends become like family – thank you Helen Wedgewood for all of the babysitting, which helped get this book finished on time. Thank you to my mum and dad and my twin Jody for all of your support. Thank you to Clare Shaw, the best friend any poet could wish for. There are so many people I've met along the way – poets, musicians, runners and readers who I've talked about, laughed about and raged about sexism with. I can't list you all here, but I was talking to you whilst I was writing, and sometimes I could hear you singing and writing back. Thank you to my family – especially my mum and dad and my twin sister Jody, and my husband – for all of the conversations over the years. Finally, I want to thank my daughter Ally, who gives me the courage to keep talking about sexism in the hope that she grows up in a different world to the one I grew up in.

NOTES

DESIRE LINES: AN INTRODUCTION

1 Denzin, N.K. (1994) 'Romancing the Text: the qualitative researcher-writer-as-bricoleur'. *Bulletin of the Council for Research in Music Education*, (122) pp.15-30

2 Weinstein, D. and Weinstein, M.A. (1991) 'Georg Simmel: sociological flaneur bricoleur'. *Theory, Culture and Society*, 8 pp.151-168

3 Denzin, N.K. (1994) 'Romancing the Text: the qualitative researcher-writer-as-bricoleur'. *Bulletin of the Council for Research in Music Education*, (122) p.6

4 Barthes, R. (1975) *The Pleasure of the Text*. New York: Hill and Wang. p.4

5 Berger, J. (1972) *Ways of Seeing*. London: Penguin. p.16

6 Ibid. p.29

7 Salih, S. (2004) *The Judith Butler Reader*. Salih, S. (ed.) Oxford: Blackwell Publishing. p.12

8 Ibid. p.4

9 Butler, J. (2000) Changing the subject: Judith Butler's politics of radical resignification. In: Olson, G.A. and Worsham, L. *The Judith Butler Reader*. pp.325-356. Malden, USA: Blackwell Publishing.

10 Shklovsky, V. (1991) *Theory of prose*. Normal, Il.: Dalkey Archive Press.

11 Bennett, T. (2003) *Formalism and Marxism*. 2nd ed., London: Routledge pp.17-22

12 Gunn, Daniel. P. (1984) 'Making art strange: a commentary on defamiliarization.' *The Georgia Review*, 38, (1) pp. 25-33

13 Ahmed, S. (2017) *Living a Feminist Life*. Durham: Duke University Press. p.32

14 Ibid. p.40

15 Ibid. p.30

16 Ahmed, S. (2017) *Living a Feminist Life*. Durham: Duke University Press. p.23

17 Ibid.

18 Madison, D.S. (1999) 'Performing theory/embodied writing.' *Text and Performance Quarterly* 19 (2) pp.107-124

19 Conquergood, D. (1985) 'Performing as a moral act: ethical dimensions of the ethnography of performance.' *Literature in Performance*, 5 (2) pp.1-13

YES, I AM JUDGING YOU

20 Berger, J. (1972) *Ways of Seeing*. London: Penguin. p.9

21 Bertram, V. (2003) *Gendering Poetry: Contemporary Poetry and Sexual Politics*. London: Pandora Press. p.40

22 Butler, J. (1997) *Excitable Speech: A Politics of the Performative*. London; New York: Routledge. p.2

23 Ibid. p.5

24 Bertram, V. (2003) *Gendering Poetry: Contemporary Poetry and Sexual Politics*. London: Pandora Press. p.40

25 Lorde, A. and Ddc. (1984) *Sister Outsider: Essays and Speeches*. Freedom, Calif: The Crossing Press. p.123

26 Butler, J. (1997) *Excitable Speech: A Politics of the Performative*. London;New York;: Routledge. p.52

27 Moore, K. (2021) *All the Men I Never Married*. Bridgend: Seren.

28 hooks, b. (1989) *Talking back: thinking feminist, thinking black*. Boston, MA: South End Press p.16

29 Ibid. p.108

30 Soloway, J. (2016) *The female gaze*. Toronto International Film Festival: [Online] [Accessed on 18th October 2022] https://www.youtube.com/watch?v=pnBvppooD9I&t=10s

A PROBLEM WITH THE MALE GAZE

31 Mulvey, L. (1975) 'Visual pleasure and narrative cinema.' *Screen*, 16(3) pp.6-18

32 Ahmed, S. (2017) *Living a Feminist Life*. Durham: Duke University Press. p.37

33 Brooks, A.T. (2007) 'Feminist standpoint epistemology: building knowledge and empowerment through women's lived experience.' *In* Hesse-Biber, S.N. and Leavy, L.P. (eds.) *Feminist Research Practice: A Primer*. London: Sage Publications, pp.53-82

34 Ahmed, S. (2017) *Living a Feminist Life*. Durham: Duke University Press. p.235

35 Cohen, A. (2017) 'Not safe for work.' *The Nation*. Cultural Criticism and Analysis. September 18th edition.

36 Nussbaum, E. (2017) 'What women want on "I love Dick".' *The New Yorker*. June 19th.

37 Cohen, A. (2017) 'Not safe for work.' *The Nation*. Cultural Criticism and Analysis. September 18th edition.

38 Brooks, A.T. (2007) 'Feminist standpoint epistemology: building knowledge and empowerment through women's lived experience.' *In* Hesse-Biber, S.N. and Leavy, L.P. (eds.) *Feminist Research Practice: A Primer*. London: Sage Publications, p.63

39 Soloway, J. (2016) *The female gaze*. Toronto International Film Festival: [Online] [Accessed on 18th October 2022] https://www.youtube.com/watch?v=pnBvppooD9I&t=10s

40 Woolf, V. (1928) *A Room of One's Own*. London: Penguin Books. p.37

41 Duffy, N. (2013) *Relative Strangeness: Reading Rosmarie Waldrop*. Shearsman Books.

42 Soloway, J. (2016) *The female gaze*. Toronto International Film Festival: [Online] [Accessed on 18th October 2022] https://www.youtube.com/watch?v=pnBvppooD9I&t=10s

43 Angel, K. (2019) 'Susanna Moore's "In the cut".' *The White Review*.

44 Ibid.

MODE OF ADDRESS

45 Murphy, M. & Brown, T. (2012) 'Learning as Relational: Intersubjectivity and Pedagogy in Higher Education' *International Journal of Lifelong Education* 31:5 pp.643-654

46 Rankine, Claudia (2020) *Just Us: An American Conversation.* Great Britain: Allen Lane, 2020.

47 Tran, Diep (2022) 'What Claudia Rankine learned from talking to white people'. *Andscape* [Online] [Accessed on 18th October 2022) https://andscape.com/features/what-claudia-rankine-learned-from-talking-to-white-people/

48 Chan, M.-J. (2018) 'Towards a poetics of racial trauma: lyric hybridity in Claudia Rankine's Citizen.' *Journal of American Studies*, 52(1) pp.137

49 Rankine, C. (2015) *Citizen: An American lyric.* London: Penguin Books. p.10

50 Ibid.

51 Soloway, J. (2016)
The female gaze. Toronto International Film Festival: [Online] [Accessed on 18th October 2022]
https://www.youtube.com/watch?v=pnBvppooD9I&t=10s

52 Chan, M.-J. (2018) 'Towards a poetics of racial trauma: lyric hybridity in Claudia Rankine's *Citizen.' Journal of American Studies*, 52(1) pp.141

53 Rankine, C.(2015) *Citizen: An American Lyric.* London: Penguin Books. p.11

54 Ibid.

55 Bakare, L. 2020, 'White people can learn from it, but that's not who I'm writing for' *The Guardian*, 8th February 2020, [Online] [Accessed 8th October 2022) https://www.theguardian.com/books/2020/feb/08/danez-smith-interview-white-people-racism-homie

56 Turnnidge. S. (2019) 'Nottinghamshire Police Accused of "Victim Blaming" After Advising Women Not To Walk Alone At Night' *Huffington Post UK News* [Online] 2019 [12.11.2019] https://www.huffingtonpost.co.uk/entry/nottinghamshire-police-advice-women-walking-alone-night_uk_5ddf8ff3e4b00149f729e2d8

57 Plath, S.1981, *Collected Poems*, London, Faber and Faber, pp.173-174

58 Levertov, D. (1983) *Poems, 1960-1967*. New York: New Directions (New Directions paperbook, NDP549). p.143

59 Lorde, A. (1997) *The Collected Poems of Audre Lorde*. New York: W.W. Norton and Company.

60 Bertram, V. (2003) *Gendering Poetry: Contemporary Poetry and Sexual Politics*. London: Pandora Press. p.65

61 Rankine, C. (2015) *Citizen: An American Lyric*. London: Penguin Books. p.77

62 Berlant, L, (2014) 'Claudia Rankine by Lauren Berlant', *Bomb Magazine* [Online] [Accessed on 18th October 2022] https://bombmagazine.org/articles/claudia-rankine/

63 Ahmed, S. (2017) *Living a Feminist Life*. Durham: Duke University Press. p.23

GUILTY FOR BEING A MAN

64 Chan, M.-J. (2018) 'Towards a poetics of racial trauma: lyric hybridity in Claudia Rankine's Citizen.' *Journal of American Studies*, 52(1) pp.137

65 Lorde, A. and Ddc. (1984) *Sister Outsider: Essays and Speeches*. Freedom, Calif: The Crossing Press. p.130

66 Grillo, T. and Wildman, S.M. (1991) 'Obscuring the Importance of Race: The Implication of Making Comparisons between Racism and Sexism (Or Other -Isms)'. *Duke Law Journal*, 1991(2) pp.397-412.

67 Ahmed, S. (2017) *Living a Feminist Life*. Durham: Duke University Press. pp.162

68 Merleau-Ponty, M. and Landes, D.A. (2013) *Phenomenology of Perception*. *Routledge* Ltd. p.170

69 Irigaray, L. (2000) *to be two*. London: The Athlone Press. p.3

70 Merleau-Ponty, M. and Landes, D.A. (2013) *Phenomenology of Perception*. Routledge Ltd. p.171

SEXISM IS A SLIPPERY AND FLUID TERM

71 Bates, L. (2014) *Everyday Sexism*. London: Simon & Schuster UK Ltd. p.16

72 Ibid. p.18

73 Rich, A. (1975) Women and Honor: Some Notes on Lying. *On Lies, Secrets, and Silence: Selected Prose 1966-1978*. New York: W.W. Norton & Company. p.190

74 Gill, R. (2011) 'Sexism reloaded, or, it's time to get angry again'. *Feminist Media Studies*, 11(1) p.62

75 Orr, G. (2002) *Poetry As Survival*. Georgia: University of Georgia Press. pp.4-5

76 Ahmed, S. (2017) *Living a Feminist Life*. Durham: Duke University Press. p.94

77 Wolff, J. and Stacey, J. (2013) *Writing Otherwise: Experiments in Cultural Criticism*. Manchester: Manchester University Press. p.59

78 Brown, L.S. (1995) 'Not outside the range'. *In* Caruth, C. (ed.) *Trauma: Explorations in Memory*. London; Baltimore, Md; Johns Hopkins University Press, p.102

79 Root, M. (1992) 'Reconstructing the impact of trauma on personality'. In Brown, L. and Ballou M (eds.) *Personality and Psychopathology: Feminist Reappraisals*. New York: Guilford Press.

80 Caruth, C. (1995) *Trauma: Explorations in Memory*. London; Baltimore, Md: Johns Hopkins University Press. p.5

81 Brown, L.S. (1995) 'Not outside the range'. In Caruth, C. (ed.) *Trauma: Explorations in Memory*. London; Baltimore, Md; Johns Hopkins University Press, p.107

82 Culler, J.D. (2015) *Theory of the Lyric*. Cambridge, Massachusetts: Harvard University Press. pp.282-283

83 Ahmed, S. (2017) *Living a Feminist Life*. Durham: Duke University Press. p.32

84 Ibid.

85 Rich, A. (1975) 'Women and Honor: Some Notes on Lying'. *On Lies,*

Secrets, and Silence: Selected Prose 1966-1978. New York: W.W. Norton & Company. p.190

86 Bertram, V. (2003) *Gendering Poetry: Contemporary Poetry and Sexual Politics*. London: Pandora Press. p.7

87 Ahmed, S. (2017) *Living a Feminist Life*. Durham: Duke University Press. p.62

88 Bertram, V. (2003) *Gendering Poetry: Contemporary Poetry and Sexual Politics*. London: Pandora Press.

89 Ahmed, S. (2017) *Living a Feminist Life*. Durham: Duke University Press. p.62

90 Grillo, T. and Wildman, S.M. (1991) 'Obscuring the Importance of Race: The Implication of Making Comparisons between Racism and Sexism (Or Other -Isms)'. *Duke Law Journal*, 1991(2) p.402

LYRIC VARIATIONS (1)

91. Ibid.

92 hooks, b. (1989) *Talking back: thinking feminist, thinking black*. Boston, MA: South End Press p.129

93 Ibid.

94 Ahmed, S. (2017) *Living a feminist life*. Durham: Duke University Press.

95 Culler, J.D. (2015) *Theory of the Lyric*. Cambridge, Massachusetts: Harvard University Press. pp.260

96 Ahmed, S. (2017) *Living a Feminist Life*. Durham: Duke University Press. pp.5-6

97 Mill, J.S. (1860) 'Thoughts on poetry and its varieties'. *The Crayon*, 7(4) pp.93-97

98 Hirsch, E. (2006) *In the beginning is the relation*. The Poetry Foundation. [Online] [Accessed on 22 December] https://www.poetryfoundation.org/articles/68414/in-the-beginning-is-the-relation

99 Mill, J.S. (1860) 'Thoughts on poetry and its varieties'. *The Crayon*, 7(4) pp.93-97.

100 Hirsch, E. (2006) *In the beginning is the relation.* The Poetry Foundation. [Online] [Accessed on 22 December] https://www.poetryfoundation.org/articles/68414/in-the-beginning-is-the-relation

101 White, G.C. (2014) *Lyric Shame: The 'Lyric' Subject of Contemporary American Poetry.* Cambridge, Massachusetts, London, England: Harvard University Press.

102 Parmar, S. and Kapil, B. (2017) 'Lyric violence, the nomadic subject and the fourth space'. *Poetry London,* (Summer 2017) pp.29-32

103. Irigaray, L. (2000) *to be two.* London: The Athlone Press. p.3

104 Rich, A. (2016) *Collected Poems.* Conrad, P. (ed.) New York: W.W. Norton & Company. p.355

105 Vendler, H. (1985) 'Introduction'. *In* Vendler, H. (ed.) *The Harvard Book of Contemporary American Poetry.* Cambridge: The Belknap Press of Harvard University Press

106 Bernstein, C. (1992) *Artifice of absorption.* EPC Digital Library: [Online] [Accessed on 28 December] http://writing.upenn.edu/epc/authors/bernstein/books/artifice/

107 White, G.C. (2014) *Lyric Shame: The 'Lyric' Subject of Contemporary American Poetry.* Cambridge, Massachusetts, London, England: Harvard University Press

108 Ibid p.115

109 Ibid p.110

110 Bernstein, C. (1992) *Artifice of absorption.* EPC Digital Library:. [Online] [Accessed on 28 December] http://writing.upenn.edu/epc/authors/bernstein/books/artifice/

111 White, G.C. (2014) *Lyric Shame: The 'Lyric' Subject of Contemporary American Poetry.* Cambridge, Massachusetts, London, England: Harvard University Press. p.115

112 Rilke, R.M. (1995). *Archaic Torso of Apollo.* [Online]. www.poets.org. Available at: https://poets.org/poem/archaic-torso-apollo [Accessed 14 February 2023].

113 Culler, J.D. (2015) *Theory of the Lyric.* Cambridge, Massachusetts: Harvard University Press. p.8

114 Ibid p.18

115 Ibid pp.282-283

116 Ahmed, S. (2017) *Living a Feminist Life*. Durham: Duke University Press. p.40

117 Lanser, S.S. (2008) 'The "I" of the beholder: equivocal attachments and the limits of structuralist narratology'. *In* Rabinowitz, P.J. and Phelan, J. (eds.) *A Companion to Narrative Theory*. Oxford: Blackwell http://capitadiscovery.co.uk/mmu/items/1838498

LYRIC VARIATIONS (2)

118 Duffy, C.A. (2000) *The World's Wife: Poems*. London: Picador. pp.2-3

119 Glick, P., Lameiras, M., Fiske, S.T., Eckes, T., Masser, B., Volpato, C., Manganelli, A.M., Pek, J.C.X., et al. (2004) 'Bad but bold: ambivalent attitudes toward men predict gender inequality in 16 nations'. *Journal of Personality and Social Psychology*, 86(5) pp.713-728

120 Caruth, C. (1995) *Trauma: Explorations in Memory*. London; Baltimore, Md: Johns Hopkins University Press. p.9

121 Caruth, C. and ProQuest. (1996) *Unclaimed experience: trauma, narrative, and history*. Baltimore: Johns Hopkins University Press. p.61

122 Orr, G. (2002) *Poetry as Survival*. Georgia: University of Georgia Press.

123 Culler, J.D. (2015) *Theory of the Lyric*. Cambridge, Massachusetts: Harvard University Press. p.279

124 Ibid. p.286

125 Ibid p.295

126 Gill, R. (2011) 'Sexism reloaded, or, it's time to get angry again'. *Feminist Media Studies*, 11(1) p.62

127 Culler, J.D. (2015) *Theory of the Lyric*. Cambridge, Massachusetts: Harvard University Press. p.350

128 Forché, C. (1993) 'Introduction'. In Forché, C. (ed.) *Against Forgetting: Twentieth Century Poetry of Witness*. New York: W.W. Norton & Co, p.31

129 Ibid. p.46

130 Chan, M.-J. (2018) 'Towards a poetics of racial trauma: lyric hybridity in Claudia Rankine's *Citizen.' Journal of American Studies*, 52(1) p.141.

131 Root, M. (1992) 'Reconstructing the impact of trauma on personality'. In Brown, L. and Ballou M (eds.) *Personality and Psychopathology: Feminist Reappraisals.* New York: Guilford Press.

132 Brown, L. (1995) 'Outside the Range' *Trauma : explorations in memory.* Baltimore, Maryland: Johns Hopkins University Press

133 Love, H. (2016) 'Small change: realism, immanence, and the politics of the micro.' *Modern Language Quarterly*, 77(3) p.436

134 Goffman, Erving. (1974) *Frame Analysis: An Essay on the Organization of Experience.* Cambridge, MA: Harvard University Press.

135 Orr, G. (2002) *Poetry as survival.* Georgia: University of Georgia Press. p.51

136 Love, H. (2016) 'Small change: realism, immanence, and the politics of the micro'. *Modern Language Quarterly*, 77(3) p.427

137 Williams, W.C. (1938). *The Red Wheelbarrow.* [Online]. Poetry Foundation. Available at: https://www.poetryfoundation.org/poems/455 02/the-red-wheelbarrow [Accessed 15 February 2023]

138 Emerson, R.M. (2009) 'Ethnography, interaction and ordinary trouble'. *Ethnography*, 10(4) pp.535-548

WOMEN'S IMAGES OF MEN –
DESIRE, VULNERABILITY AND THE GAZE

139 Kent, S. and Morreau, J. (1990) 'Lighting a Candle'. *In* Kent, S. and Morreau, J. (eds.) *Women's Images of Men.* 2nd Edition ed., London: Pandora Press, p.13

140 Ibid.

141 Kent, S. (1990) 'Looking back'. *In* Kent, S. and Morreau, J. (eds.) *Women's Images of Men.* 2nd Edition ed., London: Pandora Press, p.58

142 Ibid. p.55

143 Blanchot, M. (1994) *The Work of Fire.* Meridian: crossing aesthetics. Stanford University Press.

144 Retallack, J. (2003) *The Poethical Wager*. California: University of California Press. p.11

145 Ibid.

146 Ibid. p.19

147 Blanchot, M. (1994) *The Work of Fire*. Meridian: crossing aesthetics. Stanford University Press.

148 Kent, S. (1990) 'Looking back'. *In* Kent, S. and Morreau, J. (eds.) *Women's Images of Men*. 2nd Edition ed., London: Pandora Press, pp.58

149 Parker, R. (1980) 'Women's Images of Men'. *Spare Rib*, 99 (October) p.6

150 Retallack, J. (2003) *The Poethical Wager*. California: University of California Press. p.10

151 Parker, R. (1980) 'Women's Images of Men'. *Spare Rib*, 99 (October) p.6

152 Felman, S. (1993) *What Does a Woman Want? Reading and Sexual Difference*. Maryland: Johns Hopkins University Press. p.124

153 Rich, A. (1975) Women and Honor: Some Notes on Lying. *On lies, secrets, and silence: selected prose 1966-1978*. New York: W.W. Norton & Company. p.37

154 Grahn, J. (1985) *The Work of a Common Woman* London: Onlywoman Press p.60

155 Felman, S. (1993) *What Does a Woman Want? Reading and Sexual Difference*. Maryland: Johns Hopkins University Press. p.130

156 Ibid.

157 Kent, S. (1990) 'Looking back'. *In* Kent, S. and Morreau, J. (eds.) *Women's Images of Men*. 2nd Edition ed., London: Pandora Press, p.62

158 Love, H. (2016) 'Small change: realism, immanence, and the politics of the micro'. *Modern Language Quarterly*, 77(3) p.433

159 Alford, L. (2016) '"Full/of endless distances": forms of desire in poetic attention'. *Dibur Literary Journal*, Spring (2) pp.7-17.

160 Ibid. p.12

161 White, G.C. (2014) *Lyric Shame: The "Lyric" Subject of Contemporary American Poetry*. Cambridge, Massachusetts, London, England: Harvard University Press. pp.111-15

162 Rilke, R.M. (1995). *Archaic Torso of Apollo*. [Online]. www.poets.org. Available at: https://poets.org/poem/archaic-torso-apollo [Accessed 14 February 2023].

163 White, G.C. (2014) *Lyric Shame: The "Lyric" Subject of Contemporary American Poetry*. Cambridge, Massachusetts; London, England: Harvard University Press. pp.111-15

164 Berger, J. (1972) *Ways of Seeing*. London: Penguin. p.54

DOING GENDER

165 Butler, J. (2002) *Gender Trouble: Tenth Anniversary Edition*. Routledge Ltd. pp.43-45

166 Moore, K (2021) *All the Men I Never Married*. Bridgend: Seren. p.17

167 Angel, K. (2019b) *Daddy Issues*. London: Peninsula Press. p.111

168 Butler, J. (2002) *Gender Trouble: Tenth Anniversary Edition*. Routledge Ltd. p.178

169 Butler, J. (2005) *Giving An Account of Oneself*. New York: Fordham University Press.

170 Ibid. p.21

171 Ibid. p.51

172 Ibid. p.27

173 Ibid. p.38

174 Ibid. p.192

175 Ibid. p.27

176 Salih, S. (2004) *The Judith Butler Reader*. Salih, S. (ed.). Oxford, UK: Blackwell Publishing. p.59

177 Leonard, L.W. (2015) *52 Men*. Pasadena, CA: Red Hen Press.

178 Berger, J. (1972) *Ways of Seeing*. London: Penguin.

THE BODY IS THE BLINDSPOT OF SPEECH

179 Butler, J. (1997) *Excitable Speech: A Politics of the Performative*. London; New York: Routledge. p.11

180 Angel, K. (2021) *Tomorrow Sex Will Be Good Again* (2022) London: Verso. p.13

181 Barthes, R. (1990) *A Lover's Discourse: Fragments*. Harmondsworth: Penguin. p.101

182 Ibid. p.102

183 Ibid. pp.13-14

184 Irigaray, L. (2000) *to be two*. London: The Athlone Press. p.3

185 Barthes, R. (1990) *A Lover's Discourse: Fragments*. Harmondsworth: Penguin. p.16

186 Ibid. p.44

187 Butler, J. (1997) *Excitable Speech: A Politics of the Performative*. London; New York: Routledge. p.5

188 Moore, K (2021) *All the Men I Never Married*. Bridgend: Seren. pp10-11

189 Butler, J. (1997) *Excitable Speech: A Politics of the Performative*. London; New York: Routledge. p.13

190 Olson, C. (1997) *Projective Verse*. Poetry Foundation [Online] [November 2022] Projective Verse by Charles Olson | Poetry Foundation

191 Moore, K. (2021) *All the Men I Never Married*. Bridgend. Seren. pp.14-15

192 Ahmed, S. (2017) *Living a Feminist Life*. Durham: Duke University Press.

193 Ibid. p.83

194 Ibid. p.68

195 Ibid. p.73

196 Ibid. p.74

197 Ibid. p.82

THE ANNIHILATION OF MEN

198 Nussbaum, M.C. (1995) 'Objectification'. *Philosophy & Public Affairs*, 24(4) p.257

199 Angel, K. (2019) *Susanna Moore's 'In the Cut'*. [Online]. The White Review. Available at: https://www.thewhitereview.org/reviews/susanna-moores-cut/ [Accessed 15th February 2023]

200 Ibid.

201 Angel, K. (2020) *Sex and self-knowledge: beyond consent*. [Online]. Verso. Available at: https://www.versobooks.com/blogs/4573-sex-and-self-knowledge-beyond-consent [Accessed 15th February 2023]

202 Ibid.

203 Ibid.

WHAT IS BETWEEN-US

204 Irigaray, L. (2000) *to be two*. London: The Athlone Press. p.41

205 Ibid. p.3

206 Cavarero, A. (2000) *Relating Narratives: Storytelling and Selfhood*. London: Routledge. p.3

207 Irigaray, L. (2000) *to be two*. London: The Athlone Press. p.37

208 Ibid.

209 Irigaray, L. (2000) *to be two*. London: The Athlone Press. p.20

210 Ibid. p.40

211 Moore, K (2021) *All the Men I Never Married*. Bridgend: Seren. pp10-11

212 Ibid. p.9

213 Ibid. p.10

214 Ibid.

215 Berger, J. (2008) *Ways of Seeing*. London: Penguin. p.54

216 Moore, K (2021) *All the Men I Never Married*. Bridgend: Seren p.31

217 Ibid. p.10

218 Berger, J. (2008) *Ways of Seeing*. London: Penguin. p.54

219 Mulvey, L. (1975) 'Visual pleasure and narrative cinema'. *Screen*, 16(3) p.11

220 Irigaray, L. (2000) *to be two*. London: The Athlone Press. p.9

CONSIDERING MEN

221 Rich, A. (1994) *What Is Found There: Notebooks on Poetry and Politics*. New York: W.W. Norton & Company

222 Ibid. p.32

223 Rich, A. (1977) Husband-Right and Father-Right. *On Lies, Secrets and Silence: Selected Prose 1966-1978*. p.215

224 Rich, A. (1994) *What Is Found There: Notebooks on Poetry and Politics*. New York: W.W. Norton & Company. p.32

225 Rich, A. (1995) *On Lies, Secrets and Silence: Selected Prose, 1966-78*. New ed., New York: W.W. Norton & Company

226 Rich, A. (2016) *Collected Poems*. Conrad, P. (ed.) New York: W.W. Norton & Company. p.4

227 Ibid. p.355

228 Rich, A. (1994) *What Is Found There: Notebooks on Poetry and Politics*. New York: W.W. Norton & Company. p.34

229 Maxwell, G. (2012) *On Poetry. Oberon masters*. London: Oberon Books. p.53

230 Bertram, V. (2003) *Gendering Poetry: Contemporary Poetry and Sexual Politics*. London: Pandora Press. p.6

231 Rich, A. (1995) *On Lies, Secrets and Silence: Selected Prose, 1966-78*. New ed., New York: W.W. Norton & Company. p.193

232 Rich, A. (2016) *Collected Poems*. Conrad, P. (ed.) New York: W.W. Norton & Company. p.234

TO GIVE AN ACCOUNT OF THE SELF

233 Barthes, R. (1990) *A Lover's Discourse: Fragments*. Harmondsworth: Penguin. p.60

234 Goo Goo Dolls. (2018) *Iris*. [Online video] [12 November 2022] https://www.youtube.com/watch?v=_HZM0QiuUS8

235 Irigaray, L. (2000) *to be two*. London: The Athlone Press. p.8

236 Butler, J. (1997) *Excitable Speech: A Politics of the Performative*. London; New York: Routledge. p.30

237 Butler, J. (2005) *Giving An Account of Oneself*. New York: Fordham University Press. p.7

238 Woolf, Virginia. (1976). *Moments of Being*. 3rd ed. London: Random House. pp.84-85

239 Butler, J. (1997) *Gibing an Account of Oneself*. New York: Fordham University Press. p.21

240 Ibid. pp.21-22

241 Rich, A. (2016) *Collected Poems*. Conrad, P. (ed.) New York: W.W. Norton & Company Inc. p.234

242 Moore, K. (2015) *The Art of Falling*. Bridgend: Seren.

243 Butler, J. (2005) *Giving an Account of Oneself*. New York: Fordham University Press. p.12

244 Wolff, J. and Stacey, J. (2013) *Writing Otherwise: Experiments in Cultural Criticism*. Manchester: Manchester University Press. p.59

245 Wordsworth, W., Coleridge. S.T. (1800). *Lyrical Ballads*. Abingdon,: Oxon: Routledge. pp.190-195

246 Culler, J.D. (2015) *Theory of the Lyric*. Cambridge, Massachusetts: Harvard University Press. p.350

247 Butler, J. (2005) *Giving an Account of Oneself*. New York: Fordham University Press. p.6

248 Ibid. p.40

249 Ibid. p.56

250 Rich, A. (1972) 'When we dead awaken: writing as re-vision'. *College English*, 34(1) p.35

251 Yorke, L. (1997) *Adrienne Rich: Passion, Politics and the Body*. London: Sage Publications. p.11

VARIATIONS ON A CONCLUSION

252 Angel, K. (2020) *Sex and self-knowledge: beyond consent. Sex and self-knowledge: beyond consent*. [Online]. Verso. Available at: https://www.versobooks.com/blogs/4573-sex-and-self-knowledge-beyond-consent [Accessed 15th February 2023].

CODA: ON WAYS OF LOOKING

253 Barthes, R. (1982) *Camera lucida : reflections on photography*. London: Cape.

254 Ibid.

255 Glick, P., Lameiras, M., Fiske, S.T., Eckes, T., Masser, B., Volpato, C., Manganelli, A.M., Pek, J.C.X., et al. (2004) 'Bad but bold: ambivalent attitudes toward men predict gender inequality in 16 nations'. *Journal of Personality and Social Psychology*, 86(5) pp.713-728

256 Ahmed, S. (2017) *Living a Feminist Life*. Durham: Duke University Press. p.23

257 Koch, K. (1997) *One Train*. Manchester: Carcanet Press

258 Barthes, R. (1982) *Camera lucida: reflections on photography*. London: Cape.

259 Bishop, E. (1983) *Complete Poems*. London: Chatto & Windus. p.23